OSPREY AIRCRAFT OF THE ACES • 110

# Austro-Hungarian Albatros Aces of World War 1

SERIES EDITOR: TONY HOLMES

OSPREY AIRCRAFT OF THE ACES • 110

# Austro-Hungarian Albatros Aces of World War 1

Paolo Varriale

OSPREY
PUBLISHING

**Front Cover**
**With the engine in his flying boat
(Macchi L.3 4842) having boiled
over after its radiator was holed by
machine gun fire, Marinaio Luigi
Bruzzone attempts to hastily alight
near the northern Italian coastal
town of Porto Baseleghe in order
to seek the protection of naval
pontoons moored in the area.
Bruzzone and his observer,
Sottotenente di Vascello Luigi
D'Orso, were hoping that anti-aircraft
fire from weapons on the pontoons
would drive off the Albatros D III
patrol from *Flik* 41/J that had
targeted his flying boat during the
afternoon of 5 November 1917. The
fighters were being led by ranking
Austro-Hungarian ace Hptm Godwin
Brumowski, who was at the controls
of his distinctively marked Albatros
D III 153.45, complete with its
gruesome black-shrouded skull
insignia.**

**The crew of L.3 4842, assigned to
*251ª Squadriglia* and flying from the
nearby Venice Seaplane Station, had
just dropped a message over
Portogruaro when they were
attacked by aces Brumowski and
Oberleutnante Frank Linke-Crawford
and Rudolf von Szepessy-Sokoll.
Both Bruzzone and D'Orso escaped
unhurt from the flying boat and were
soon rescued by Italian naval vessels.**

**A few minutes before 4842's
demise, Brumowski and his
colleagues had downed another L.3
from *251ª Squadriglia*. The flying
boat had been intercepted while
bombing newly built bridges across
the Tagliamento River – these had
been constructed by Austro-
Hungarian engineers. The L.3 duly
crashed in a swamp, killing the pilot,
Tenente Arnaldo De Filippis (who was
commanding officer of *251ª
Squadriglia*), and his observer
Tenente di Vascello Francesco Cappa,
whose father was a serving admiral
(*Cover artwork by Mark
Postlethwaite*)**

First published in Great Britain in 2012 by Osprey Publishing
Midland House, West Way, Botley, Oxford, OX2 0PH
44-02 23rd Street, Suite 219, Long Island City, NY, 11101, USA

E-mail; info@ospreypublishing.com

Osprey Publishing is part of the Osprey Group

A CIP catalogue record for this book is available from the British Library

ISBN: 978 1 84908 747 6
PDF e-book ISBN: 978 1 84908 748 3
ePub ISBN: 978 1 78096 115 6

Edited by Philip Jarrett and Tony Holmes
Cover artwork by Mark Postlethwaite
Aircraft profiles by Harry Dempsey
Index by Alan Thatcher
Originated by PDQ Digital Media Solutions, UK
Printed in China through Bookbuilders

12 13 14 15 16 17    10 9 8 7 6 5 4 3 2 1

Osprey Publishing is supporting the Woodland Trust, the UK's leading woodland conservation charity, by funding the dedication of trees.

**www.ospreypublishing.com**

ACKNOWLEDGEMENTS

The author wishes to thank the friends and fellow historians who helped with this work. In joint 'first place' are Gregory Alegy, who revised the English manuscript, and Ivo Michael Forti, who translated the German documents. Invaluable help came from Mauro Antonellini, Vinko Avsenak, Tenente Colonnello Massimiliano Barlattani, Jerzy Butkiewicz, Boris Ciglic, Herman Dekker, Generale Basilio Di Martino, Rudolf Höfling, Antonio Iozzi, Andrew Kemp, Bohumir Kudlicka, the late Carlo Lucchini, Koloman Mayrhofer, Paolo Miana, Karl Meindl, Tenente Colonnello Giancarlo Montinaro, Miroslav Pokorny, Jiri Railich, Matjaz Ravbar, Colonnello Roberto Sardo, Johannes Valenta and, last but certainly not least, Greg VanWyngarden.

# CONTENTS

# A LONG-AWAITED FIGHTER

'One of our pilots shot down an enemy biplane in an aerial fight near San Lorenzo di Mossa, where the Italian aeroplane was destroyed by our artillery.'

These few lines in the *Heeresbericht* (Austro-Hungarian Army Bulletin) mark the first official aerial victory by an Austro-Hungarian fighter, on 25 November 1915. The aircraft that shot down the Italian biplane of *11ª Squadriglia* Farman were an Albatros B I biplane and one of the two Fokker A III monoplanes (the Austrian designation for E I) recently delivered from Germany to *Fliegerkompagnie* 4 (Air Company, or *Flik*) on the Italian Front. The Fokker was piloted by Hptm Mathias Bernath.

The number of aeroplanes on the Italian Front increased over coming weeks, and in February 1916 the monoplanes were gathered into a provisional fighter unit named *Fokker-Kampfstaffeln* or *Fokker Alarm-Bereitschaft* (Fokker Alarm Detachment), the first *Luftfahrtruppen* (Aviation Troop, *LFT*) unit to be given such specialised duties.

Apart from their synchronised Spandau machine guns, the Fokker monoplanes were lacking in several respects, but their day of glory came on 18 February 1916, when the first true fighter in history met one of the first true bombers. On that day the Italians sent a group of Caproni 300 hp twin-engined biplanes to attack Ljubljana in retaliation for the raids on their cities, unaware of the arrival of the Fokkers. The bombers crossed the lines individually, and near the Ternova Wood Ca.478 was attacked by the Fokkers of Bernath and Hptm Heinrich Korstba, who emptied their machine gun belts into the target. Two of the three Italian airmen, Maggiore Alfredo Barbieri and Capitano Luigi Bailo, commanding officer of the *1ª Squadriglia da Offesa*, were killed, but the survivor, Capitano Oreste Salomone, was able to bring the aeroplane limping back to an Italian airfield. He was subsequently awarded the *Medaglia d'Oro al Valor Militare* for his efforts, thus becoming the first member of the Italian air service to receive the highest Italian award for military gallantry.

However, the Capronis' ordeal was not over. On the way back from the target Ca.703 also ran into the Austro-Hungarian fighters, which had had time to land in Ajsevica, refuel and rearm, and take off again. According to the late Dr Martin O'Connor, Hptm Heinrich Korstba, who was flying Fokker 03.51 during the combat, wrote in his report;

'I reached a height of 2700 m [8860 ft] and dived on a Caproni, which was flying at 2600 m [8530 ft]. I fired about 150 rounds from a distance of less than 80 m [260 ft]. He turned into me and fired at me with a machine gun from in front of and below me [the ribs and covering fabric of 03.51 were shot through]. I fired the rest of my ammunition at the rear of the enemy from about 40 m [130 ft]. At this moment Oblt Hautzmayer dived on him skilfully and shot him again. I flew on the Caproni's right flank and prevented his escape by changing my course. Over Prvazina the other Albatros and Fokker aircraft overtook the Caproni. I do not wish to belittle the contribution of our other aircraft, and I emphasise that, were I alone, the Caproni would have slipped across the frontline, because I fired all of my ammunition and was now out of fuel.'

Aboard the Italian bomber, Capitano Tullio Visconti had been killed trying to defend the aeroplane, and his colleague, Capitano Gaetano Turilli, could only crash-land the riddled Caproni in a field near Merna, in enemy territory. The bomber was recovered and repaired, later flying with the serial 00.52 from Aspern airfield, where it was found by its former owners in November 1918 after the Armistice.

Despite this exploit the Fokker A III soon became outdated, especially when faced by the increasing number of new Nieuport 11 fighters being fielded by the air service of the *Regio Esercito* (Italian Army). The Germans were unable to help their ally by supplying their new fighters, but the *LFT* believed it had the right aeroplane in the form of the new Brandenburg D I, commonly known as the KD (*Kampfdoppeldecker*; combat biplane) and nicknamed *Spinne* (spider) owing to the arrangement of its interplane struts. Operational trials of the D I carried out by *Flik* 26 on the Eastern Front gave rise to high expectations, and on 25 August 1916 an order for 50 was placed. According to *Austro-Hungarian Army Aircraft of World War One*, by Peter Grosz, George Haddow and Peter Schiemer, Oberst Emil Uzelac, commander of the *LFT*, was pleased to be able to inform his staff that 'The Fokker fighter is outdated, therefore I have authorised the production of a light biplane fighter that is equal to all combat requirements'.

Unfortunately his trust was misplaced, because the first Austro-Hungarian fighter to be built in quantity proved a great and painful disappointment for the men of the *LFT* and their leader from the very start of its operational use in the autumn of 1916. When reports of the KD's bad performance became to arrive in the office of the Kommandant of the *LFT*, Uzelac began visiting the frontline units to learn more. On 7 November 1916 he arrived at the airfield of *Flik* 19, whose commander, Oberst Adolf Heyrowsky, had grounded all the D Is, awaiting further instructions. As usual for Uzelac, this was a surprise visit, and Heyrowsky was away, but the *Koluft* decided to test the aeroplane himself. Having no respect for rank, the KD also tried to kill the senior officer, who luckily suffered only concussion when the aircraft crashed.

At this time the *Flik* were still not specialised, and their inventories included different aeroplanes for different tasks, but in the spring of 1917 the *LFT* created two pure fighter units on the Italian Front, *Flik* 41/J and 42/J ('J' for *Jagd*, fighter), and equipped them with the KD.

Even though the KDs built by Phönix were slightly better than the original ones produced by Hansa-Brandenburg, there were general complaints about the type's poor ceiling and tricky flying characteristics, it being prone to enter a sudden spin which left inexperienced pilots with little hope of regaining control. The previously mentioned book quotes a discouraging number of adverse opinions of the D I from units that used it. *Flik* 23 wrote that 'In the pilots' unanimous opinion, they cannot give full attention to the combat

The Austro-Hungarian pilot's badge is visible on the tunic of Oblt Godwin Brumowski, who is standing in front of the peculiar interplane struts of a *Flik* 41 Brandenburg D I in this photograph, taken before May 1917 – the month in which he was promoted to hauptmann. The *LFT's* most successful ace started his career as a fighter pilot, and obtained 18 of his confirmed victories with this very demanding aeroplane *(Vinko Avsenak)*

The Albatros fighter's elegant lines were enhanced by the Oeffag company's renowned woodworking skills. The D III production prototype 53.21 made its maiden flight in February 1917 from Wiener-Neustadt airfield. In this photograph the aeroplane has the winter cowling fitted over the cylinder heads, and the machine guns have not yet been installed. In September 1917 the aircraft was flown by StFw Friedrich Hefty, and it then moved to the *Feldfliegerschule* in Campoformido, where it crashed on 4 June 1918 with the loss of the pilot, Oblt Otto Patz – a former observer from *Flik 2* (*via Author*)

at hand if they are so totally occupied with controlling the aircraft. In addition, the climb is so slow that the fighter must take off well before our observation aircraft in order to reach escort altitude. The KD's ceiling is much inferior to that of enemy Nieuports, which generally operate between 4000 and 5000 m [13,000 and 16,000 ft]'.

*Flik* 41/J echoed these words, stating 'The KD is absolutely useless. The best pilots (and only they can fly the type) are shackled, ruin their nerves and perish in the crashes over the airfield, without their expert skill achieving anything'. In more direct terms, pilots simply called the KD the *'fliegende Sarg'* (flying coffin) or *'Totschläger'* (killer).

Some of the very best pilots were able to achieve combat victories, almost all on Phönix-built examples, and future top aces such as Arigi, Brumowski, Fiala, Linke-Crawford and Kiss enjoyed success with the KD despite is unenviable reputation. The *LFT* had to fight on with this unpopular aircraft until it was replaced by a new fighter. Luckily, the substitute would be far better.

In August 1916 – the same month in which Uzelac had praised the KD – news of the accomplishments of the Albatros D I and D II fighters began to arrive in Vienna, following their successful operational debut with the German *Jagdstaffeln* (fighter squadrons) on the Western Front. Bad reports about the KD had increased alarmingly, and the Austro-Hungarian aircraft manufacturers, together with the *LFT*, hastened to acquire production rights for the D II and the new D III. The obvious candidate to undertake production was the Oesterr.-Ungarische Albatros Flugzeugwerke AG (Phönix Flugzeugwerke AG from February 1917), which was linked to the German parent firm, but the licence was refused because the factory was still engaged in KD production.

Moreover, the War Ministry tried to oppose the concentration of orders in the firms owned by Austrian entrepreneur Camillo Castiglioni. Castiglioni was also detested by Uzelac, who proposed that his Navy deferment be revoked in order to draft him and send him to the *Orientkorps* in Palestine, probably regretting that there was nowhere more distant.

Consequently, the licence was granted to the Oesterreichische Flugzeugfabrik AG (Oeffag), which up to then had built C I and C II reconnaissance aircraft for the *LFT* and K-type seaplanes for the *K u K Kriegsmarine*. On 4 December 1916 the first order for the new aircraft was signed, comprising 16 Albatros D IIs and 34 D IIIs at a price of 30,500 *Kronen* each, without engines. After a successful static-load test on the lower wing, production was shifted to the D III, with the D II

"PILOTENRAUM"

The breech of a single Schwarzlose machine gun protrudes into the cockpit of this early Albatros. On the right is a Wilhel Morell Phylax tachometer, and beneath it is a bank indicator, while on the left is an altimeter, also built by Morell. In the lower right corner a Bosch magneto with its crank is visible. The handgrip of the control column already has the trigger for the second machine gun (Koloman Mayrhofer)

order being reduced to just four airframes. The D IIs were numbered 53.01 to 53.16 and the D IIIs were 53.20-53.53.

Engineers from the Stadlau firm did not simply produce a slavish imitation of the German D III, but strengthened the lower wings to eliminate the recurring wing-flutter failures that were the Achilles' heel of the original design. Almost dimensionally identical to their German counterparts, Austrian-built D IIs and D IIIs had a 185 hp Austro-Daimler engine instead of the original 160 hp Mercedes. Although it was heavier, the more powerful engine gave the Viennese breed a better rate of climb and a speed increase of about 15 km/h (9 mph) over the original fighter.

The first machine, 53.01, made its maiden flight in January 1917, 53.20 first flew in mid-February and the *LFT* commenced acceptance trials in May for both versions. That same February a second batch of 11 fighters (53.54-53.64) was ordered at a cost of 33,500 *Kronen* per aircraft, excluding engines and armament.

The nose of the Albatros fighter could house two Schwarzlose machine guns (the standard weapon of the Austro-Hungarian Army), which was able to fire its 8 mm bullets at 572 m/sec at a rate of 350-430 rounds per minute. For aerial use the original Modell M 7/12 had the water jacket cut open or removed altogether. The following version, developed by Steyr as the M 16 in mid-1916, lacked the heavy jacket from the outset, and its rate of fire was increased to 560-580 rounds per minute. However, this was reduced by the synchronisation system.

As with other air forces involved in the war, the *LFT* had to develop ammunition to suit the peculiar nature of air combat. The Schwarzlose guns installed in the aircraft used the usual mix of incendiary, tracer, explosive and armour-piercing bullets, but only in late 1918, with the introduction of SP and XX ammunition, did *LFT* airmen finally have an effective weapon. By this time it was simply too late.

The *LFT* was constantly plagued by a shortage of synchronisation devices owing to the scarcity of the precision tools necessary for their production. As a result, it was often obliged to accept aircraft unarmed and send them to the frontline units, where the armourers installed machine guns and synchronisation systems. Several makeshift solutions were tested in the field, as depicted in many photographs. These ranged from a machine gun installed on the upper wing centre-section and angled to fire outside the propeller arc, to weapons mounted on a pillar on the fuselage side and angled to fire outboard.

It seems that most of the early Albatros fighters built for the *LFT* were fitted with devices developed in 1916 by the technical officer of *Flik* 8, Ltn Otto Bernatzik, which had a peculiar and irregular firing cadence with a high-rpm engine. The aircraft then began to receive the Daimler Geared Synchronisation that had been specially designed for twin machine guns, the device firing an alternate weapon at every second propeller revolution. It was not possible to fire the Schwarzlose M 7/12 with the engine idling, but there were no restrictions for the M 16 gun. Finally, in 1918, the system developed by Oblt Guido Priesel and tested for the first time on a D III in October 1917 became standard equipment for Albatros fighters.

Oblt Göttl smiles in front of D III 53.70. This aeroplane was accepted by the *LFT* in July 1917 and delivered to *Flik* 17/D, and it subsequently served with several units. The fighter's last known duty was as a trainer in *Flik* 3/J. It is in mostly a plain finish, but the rudder appears to be camouflaged and the tail painted a darker colour *(Boris Ciglic)*

The aeroplanes were soon sent to operational zones, with most of the D IIs being sent to the Russian Front, where the enemy threat was of less concern. Here, they served in *Flik* 3, 5, 7, 10, 14, 20, 22, 25, 26 and 37, while most of the D IIIs were sent to oppose the more active Italian air force.

Frontline pilots welcomed the arrival of the aircraft as a definite sign of progress, as they finally had an aeroplane that put them on a par with enemy fighters, being as fast as the hated KD but with a better rate of climb and superior manoeuvrability. Above all, it had none of the KD's vicious habits when aloft.

The Oeffag company's skill in shaping the plywood fuselage was superb, and this, together with the capabilities of its expert workers, created one of the nicest aeroplanes ever built, and the airframe was strong enough to take engines of greater power as soon as they became available. The 200 hp Austro-Daimler engine fitted perfectly into the fighter, and the series 153, so named according to the *LFT* designation system, was initially ordered as a first batch of 61 (153.01-153.61) on 3 February 1917, followed by a second of 50 (153.62-153.111) in July, a third of 100 (153.112-153.211) in October and a fourth (153.212-153.281) in May 1918.

Six Albatros D IIIs of Alarm Bereitschaft Pergine in the summer of 1917, with the village of Roncogno as a backdrop. The unit marked its aircraft with several colours. The noses, struts and wheel discs on the first and second fighters are painted white, while multiple sources attest that the darker colour seen on the other machines could be red, yellow or black on individual fighters. This narrow airfield was still in use for sport aircraft until several years ago, when a main road and an industrial area were built on the site *(Koloman Mayrhofer)*

The crowded production hall of the Oeffag factory in June 1917. Barely visible in the foreground is the Oeffag reconnaissance two-seater prototype 50.09. Behind it, several Series 153 Albatros await final fitting-out. The first aeroplanes of the type were accepted by the *LFT* in July. D III 153.04 was subsequently used by Oblt Frank Linke-Crafword to obtain his fifth confirmed victory on 23 September *(Greg VanWyngarden)*

From aircraft 153.112 the fuselage outline changed, the propeller spinner being left off to give a rounded nose. Several earlier aircraft had the spinner removed because of its tendency to come off in flight, which could damage the airframe. As an additional benefit the new version gained a speed increment of about 14 km/h (9 mph).

The new version was again praised by military pilots in both test and operational flights. According to Aharon Tesar's book devoted to the fighter, StFw Friedrich Hefty stated that the 153-series Albatros was 'an aeroplane of an excellent design, perfectly balanced and especially fit for aerobatics. Its climbing capacity equalled that of Hanriots and [Sopwith] Camels, but its horizontal speed was lower than that of SPADs'.

The improved Austro-Daimler engine, with an output of 225 hp, was also fitted, creating the 253 series, the last version of this pugnacious fighter. The order for the first 230 aircraft (253.01-253.230) was signed in May 1918, on the same day as the last batch of 153s was ordered.

The judgment was unanimous. 'Unquestionably the most manoeuvrable and safest fighter at the Front. It has the pilots' complete trust. Because of its excellent handling and performance, it is preferred over every other fighter. Mass production is urgent'. In August a final order for a batch of 100 (253.231-253.330) was signed, but in spite of this excellent aircraft and the desperate courage of the *K u K* airmen, the days of the old empire were numbered. At the end of the war it appears that work on the last batch of D IIIs continued up to the fuselage of 253.260. Altogether, between May 1917 and October 1918 the *LFT* took delivery of 16 D IIs Series 53, 44 D IIIs Series 53.2, 281 D IIIs Series 153 and 201 D IIIs Series 253 from Oeffag, making a total of 542 machines.

In 1977 Martin O'Connor asked Julius Arigi to compare the Austro-Hungarian fighters, the ace noting;

'The Phönix fighters were the most sturdily built. They were very solid and dependable. You paid a price for this because they were less manoeuvrable and climbed more poorly. They were excellent in a dive since you could dive them as fast as you wanted without fear of tearing their wings off.

'The Berg (Aviatik D I) was the opposite of the Phönix. It was light and extremely manoeuvrable, but was weakly built. There was a great tendency for the parts to bend and for the aircraft to actually lose wing and tail sections during violent manoeuvring or even in a not-too-steep dive. The Bergs shed their wing fabric fairly easily.

'The Albatros was almost the exact middle of the road in all aspects between the Phönix and the Berg.'

The Armistice did not signal the end of aerial combats in which the D III was involved, as several served in the air service of the Austrian *Volskwehr* during the Carinthian War, which continued through to mid-1919, and 38 brand new Series 253s were used by the newly born Polish Air Force against Soviet Russia. The first batch of 17 aeroplanes arrived in Poland in the summer of 1919, and in August 12 were assigned to *7. Eskadra Lotnicza* (7th Air Squadron) based at Lvov-Lewandovska airfield. The American volunteers in Poland were gathered in this unit, and in November Maj Cedric Fauntleroy became commanding officer of what would soon be called *Eskadra Kosciuszkovska* (Kosciuszko Squadron), named after the Polish hero Tadeusz Kosciuszko, who fought in the American Revolutionary War. Among its pilots was World War 1 veteran Capt Merian Caldwell Cooper, who would later direct the film *King Kong*.

The unit adopted as its insignia a *Czapka*, the distinctive Polish cavalry headgear, with crossed scythes on a field of 13 stars, thus combining Polish and American symbols, and made its operational debut in April 1920 during the Kiev Offensive, flying Albatros and Italian-built Ansaldo A 1 fighters. Owing to the lack of air opposition the aircraft were used to strafe ground targets at low level, mainly being directed against Semyon Budionny's First Cavalry Army. The Albatros also served under the Polish flag in the *2. Wielkopolska Eskadra,* which, due to the arrival of the new aeroplanes, changed its name to *13. Eskadra Myśliwska* (13th Fighter Squadron).

A small number of D IIs and D IIIs were also used by private owners. One such machine belonged to Julius Arigi, and it had the words *Ikarus* and *Mopsi* painted on its fuselage sides, but it crashed on 23 May 1921, killing *Flik* 7 veteran Gottfried Russ.

Hard times were coming, and Oeffag was unable to survive the post-war crisis. In 1935 the factory was sold to the newly established Wiener-Neustädter Flugzeugfabrik. During World War 2 the plant returned to the construction of first-rate aircraft, being involved in the mass production of Messerschmitt fighters. As a main target of the Allied strategic bombing campaign, the Oeffag buildings were badly damaged. What survived through to VE-Day was subsequently levelled by the Red Army after the war had ended.

Although several parts from original Albatros fighters are held by museums, especially in Italy, no complete aircraft have survived. However, the breed has recently been reborn in Austria in the workshop of Kraftlab, where Koloman Mayrhofer and his staff are building a small number of painstakingly accurate flying reproductions. The first of these machines has received the serial 253.24 and is marked up in the colours of a fighter flown by Fiala von Fernbrugg in the summer of 1918. This reproduction, which has been fitted with an original 225 hp Austro-Daimler engine built in 1918, made its first flight at Oberschleissheim airfield near Munich on 10 April 2012 in the hands of French test pilot Roger-Louis Texier.

# THE AUSTRO-HUNGARIAN AIR FORCE IN WORLD WAR 1 – A BRIEF OVERVIEW

The Austro-Hungarian air force entered the conflict with a few machines of uncertain reliability, the best of which were of German origin. It suffered from the pre-war inertia and distrust of the Ministry of War, despite the support of Chief of Staff Franz Conrad von Hötzendorf and the considerable efforts of the tireless Oberst Uzelac.

The Hapsburg Empire was an industrially backward state, and for the duration of the war the development of the aviation industry was greatly hampered by asphyxiating bureaucratic fetters, shortsighted industrial policies, poor choices, lack of funds and an ever-increasing shortage of raw materials. Not only did the few valid projects suffer constant delays, but aircraft production never reached a satisfactory output, nor an adequate quality standard.

In spite of that, the Austro-Hungarian airmen never pulled back until the last, paying a heavy toll against an opponent who daily grew more powerful, skilful and expert.

At the outbreak of war the Austro-Hungarian air force was still forming, yet it was still able to send 13 *Flik* to the front. Engaged on the Russian and Balkan Fronts, the airmen from these units were able to gain early combat experience. However, the strategic situation changed when, on the Southwestern Front, Italy decided to enter the war on the *Entente* side on 24 May 1915. In response, the *Kriegministerium* (War Ministry) sent both *Flik* 12 and 16, which had been kept as reserve, to the new front, where they were joined by four more units in June.

On 23 June – the day of the first Italian offensive on the Isonzo – the order of battle of Austro-Hungarian aviation on that front was as follows;

| Unit | Airfield | Commanding Officer | Aeroplanes |
|------|----------|--------------------|------------|
| *Flik* 2 | Ajdussina | Hptm Ferdinand Cavallar Ritter von Grabensprung | 2 Aviatik B Is, 2 Lloyd C Is |
| *Flik* 4 | Ajsevica | Hptm Mathias Bernath | 1 Rumpler B I, 3 Lloyd C Is |
| *Flik* 8 | Altura | Hptm Gustav Studeny | 5 Albatros B Is |
| *Flik* 12 | St Veit | Hptm Rudolf Klöpp | 2 Lohner B IIIs, 1 Lohner B IV |

Following Italy's declaration of war against the Austro-Hungarians, the air force was reorganised in July 1915. As part of this process, its name was changed from *Luftfahrschifferabteilung* (Aviation Detachment) to *Luftfahrtruppen* (Aviation Troops).

Taking advantage of ten months of operations, and of the Italian air service's absolute lack of preparation, the *LFT* was very active from the beginning – not only in terms of generating flights over the front, but also in carrying out long-range missions such as the raids on Milan and other cities in northern Italy at the beginning of 1916. These attacks worried the population and caused quite a stir within the Italian High Command.

Hitherto strictly on the defensive, in May 1916 the Austro-Hungarians launched the *Strafexpedition* (Punitive Expedition) offensive in the northern sector of the front against its former ally. *Heeresgruppe* (Army Group) GO *Erzherzog Eugen* had the following aircraft assigned to it;

| Unit | Airfield | Commanding Officer | Aeroplanes |
|---|---|---|---|
| *Flik* 7 | Pergine | Hptm Bruno Schonowsky | 4 Lohner B VIIs, 2 Brandenburg C Is |
| *Flik* 8 | Pergine | *Rittmeister* Georg Edler von Lehmann | 3 Lohner B VIIs, 2 Brandenburg C Is |
| *Flik* 15 | Pergine | Hptm Karl Christian | 2 Brandenburg C Is, 5 Lloyd C IIIs |
| *Flik* 17 | Gardolo | Hptm Eugen Steinner-Göltl | 4 Lohner B VIIs, 1 Lloyd C II |
| *Flik* 21 | Gardolo | Hptm Walter Lux Edler von Trurecht | 2 Brandenburg C Is, 5 Lloyd C IIIs |
| *Flik* 23 | Gardolo | Hptm Heinrich Kostrba | 2 Brandenburg C Is, 6 Lloyd C IIIs |
| *Flik* 24 | Pergine | Hptm Gustav Studeny | 4 Brandenburg C Is |

In the spring of 1916 the slight technical superiority over Italian aviation that the *LFT* had enjoyed at the beginning of war began to be eroded by the new aircraft fielded by the enemy, which also demonstrated an ability to learn quickly how to exploit the capabilities of the new mounts.

While the pressure exerted on the *LFT* by its adversaries increased slowly but steadily, at the end of October the Austro-Hungarian order of battle along the Isonzo Front was as follows:

| Unit | Airfield | Commanding Officer | Aeroplanes |
|---|---|---|---|
| *Flik* 2 | Ajdussina | *Rittmeister* Eugen Graf Somssich de Saard | 6 Brandenburg C Is |
| *Flik* 4 | Wippach | Oblt Alfons Veljacic | 5 Brandenburg C Is |
| *Flik* 12 | Wippach | Hptm Arpad Gruber | 5 Brandenburg C Is |
| *Flik* 19 | Ajdussina | Hptm Adolf Heyrowsky | 4 Brandenburg C Is, 2 Fokker A IIIs |
| *Flik* 23 | Prosecco | Hptm Heinrich Kostrba | 7 Brandenburg C Is |
| *Flik* 28 | Prosecco | Hptm Viktor Schünzel | 5 Brandenburg C Is |
| *Flik* 34 | Podagra | Hptm Karl Sabeditsch | 4 Brandenburg C Is, 1 Lloyd C III |

After the winter pause the fighting flared up again, and in the spring and summer of 1917 the Italian Head of Staff, Generale Luigi Cadorna, launched a huge offensive in another of the countless attempts to break the Isonzo Front.

On 18 August 1917 the *Isonzoarmee* had the following types on strength;

| Unit | Airfield | Commanding officer | Aeroplanes |
|---|---|---|---|
| *Flik* 2 | Veldes | *Rittmeister* Eugen Graf Sommsich de Saard | 4 Brandenburg C Is |
| *Flik* 4 | Wippach | Hptm Oskar Lestin | 5 Brandenburg C Is, 1 Brandenburg D I |
| *Flik* 12 | Wippach | Hptm Arpad Gruber | 6 Brandenburg C Is, 1 Brandenburg D I |
| *Flik* 19 | Ajdussina | Hptm Karl Heyrowsky | 8 Brandenburg C Is, 1 Aviatik C I, 1 Albatros D III |
| *Flik* 23 | Divaccia | *Rittmeister* Wilhelm Graf Kolowrat-Kalowski-Liebstein | 5 Brandenburg C Is 1 Aviatik C I, 2 Brandenburg D Is |
| *Flik* 28 | Prosecco | Oblt Alexander Hartzer | 6 Brandenburg C Is |
| *Flik* 32 | St Veit | Hptm Richard Hübner | 4 Brandenburg C Is, 1 Brandenburg D I |
| *Flik* 34 | Podagra | Hptm Vinzenz Martinek | 5 Brandenburg C Is, 1 Aviatik C I, 1 Brandenburg D I, 1 Albatros D II |

| Flik 35 | St Veit | Hptm Eduard Rzmenowski von Trautenegg | 9 Brandenburg C Is |
| Flik 41/J | Sesana | Hptm Godwin Brumowski | 4 Brandenburg D Is |
| Flik 42/J | Sesana | Hptm Ladislaus Hary | 5 Brandenburg D Is 6 Albatros D IIIs |
| Flik 46/F | Divaccia | Hptm Karl Banfield | 5 Brandenburg C Is, 2 Brandenburg D Is, 1 Albatros D III |
| FlG I | Divaccia | Hptm Karl Sabeditsch | 8 Brandenburg C Is, 2 Brandenburg D Is, 2 Aviatik D Is |

During the battle two fighter units equipped with Albatros were sent to the Isonzo Front to reinforce the *Isonzoarmee*, namely *Flik* 51/J, commanded by *Rittmeister* Wedige von Froreich, and *Flik* 55/J, commanded by Oblt Josef von Maier.

An unknown artist produced this amusing watercolour caricature of Wedige von Froreich, the first commanding officer of *Flik* 51/J, who arrived at Ajdussina airfield, on the Isonzo Front, in late August 1917. Froreich claimed the unit's first victory on the 26th of that same month. The caption means 'The flying Cavalry Captain' *(Ivo Michael Forti)*

The summer offensive (the 11th Isonzo Battle) cost the Italians a 'river of blood' for little ground gained, but pushed the Hapsburg Army to the verge of collapse. To resolve this dangerous situation the Austro-Hungarians asked and obtained the help of the Germans. German and Austro-Hungarian troops came together to form the new 14th Army, which, under the command of the skilful German Gen Otto von Below, began to gather in the area of the upper Isonzo Valley. Support was also provided by some veteran German aviation units from the Western Front.

Thanks to wise planning and the bad weather that precluded effective Italian reconnaissance flights, the complex movements went unnoticed through to their completion on 10 October. The stage was now set for a major military disaster, and the introduction to history of the name of a hitherto obscure village, Caporetto (Karfreit in German and now Kobarid, in Slovenia).

On 24 October 1917 the order of battle of German and Austro-Hungarian aviation on the Isonzo Front was as follows;

Albatros D III 153.05 came to grief due to engine failure in September 1917, and it was written off the following month. The rugged terrain in the Karst region did not offer space for crash-landings, and even a little trouble could end in a total loss of an aeroplane, and possibly the pilot as well. *Flik* 41/J had a penchant for decorating its fighters with black-and-white geometric symbols, but these were not used as pilots' personal markings *(Aeronautica Militare Italiana)*

15

| Unit | Airfield | Commanding Officer |
|---|---|---|
| *K u K 1. Isonzoarmee* | | Oberstlt Hans Umlauff Ritter von Frankwell |
| *Flik* 4/D | Wippach | Hptm Oskar Lestin |
| *Flik* 23/D | Divaccia | *Rittmeister* Wilhelm Graf Kolowrat-Kakowski-Liebestein |
| *Flik* 28/D | Prosecco | Oblt Alexander Hartzer |
| *Flik* 34/D | Podagra | Hptm Vinzenz Martinek |
| *Flik* 35/D | St Veit | Hptm Eduard Rzmenowski von Trautenegg |
| *Flik* 41/J | Sesana | Hptm Godwin Brumowski |
| *Flik* 42/J | Sesana | Hptm Ladislaus Hary |
| *Flik* 46/F | Divaccia | Hptm Karl Banfield |
| *Flik* 101/G | Divaccia | Oblt Johann Löw |
| *K u K 2. Isonzoarmee* | | Hptm Adolf Heyrowsky (Temporary) |
| *Flik* 12/D | Wippach | Hptm Arpad Gruber |
| *Flik* 19/D | Ajdussina | Oblt Ludwig Hautzmayer (Temporary) |
| *Flik* 32/D | St Veit | Hptm Richard Hübner |
| *Flik* 50/D | Maria Au (near Ajdussina) | Oblt Viktor Breitenfelder |
| *Flik* 51/J | Ajdussina | *Rittmeister* Wedige von Froreich |
| *Flik* 54/D | Oberloitsch | *Rittmeister* Franz Lamprecht |
| *Flik* 55/J | Ajdussina | Oblt Josef von Maier |
| *Flik* 57/F | Oberloitsch | Hptm Karl Huppner |
| *Flik* 58/D | Ajdussina | Hptm Oskar Fekete |
| *K u K 10. Isonzoarmee* | | |
| *Flik* 16/D | Seebach | Hptm Raoul Stoisavljevic |
| *14. Armee (German)* | | Kofl Hptm von Oertzen |
| *Flik* 2/D | Veldes | Oblt August Raft Edler von Marwil |
| *Flik* 39/D | Villach | Oblt Rudolph Dworzak von Kulmburg (Temporary) |
| *Flik* 47/F | Villach | Hptm Ferdinand Cavallar Ritter von Grabensprung |
| *Flik* 53/D | Lees | Oblt Rudolf Vanicek |
| *Flik* 56/J | Villach | Oblt Robert Ellner |
| *Reihenbildzug 1* (German) | Krainburg | Oblt von Homburg |
| *Jasta* 1 (German) | Veldes | Oblt Otto Deindl |
| *Jasta* 31 (German) | Auritz | Oblt Werner Zech |
| *Jasta* 39 | Lees | Lt August Raben |
| *FFl Abt.* 14 (German) | – | – |
| *FFl Abt.* 17 (German) | St Veit | Hptm Eichhorn |
| *FFl Abt.* 39 (German) | – | Hptm Keller |
| *FFl Abt.* (A) 204 (German) | St Veit | Hptm von Hachenburg |
| *FFl Abt.* (A) 219 (German) | St Veit | Hptm Kaufmann |
| *FFl Abt.* (A) 232 (German) | St Veit | *Rittmeister* Klötzen |

The Italians not only lost the few gains on the ground achieved in two years of unspeakable suffering, but also had to retreat to the Piave River. Yet in spite of the heavy losses the *Regio Esercito* was able to hold its new line, while British and French reinforcements came to help.

Eventually, the new year that started so promisingly for the Dual Monarchy ended in defeat, its armed forces strangled by a lack of

Oblt Benno Fiala Ritter von Fernbrugg, second from right, stands to attention in front of *Kaiser* Karl I during a military ceremony, with his German pilot's badge visible under his left breast pocket. With 28 confirmed victories on the Italian Front, he ranks third in the list of Austro-Hungarian aces *(Ivo Michael Forti)*

After the 12th Battle of Isonzo the *LFT* took possession of a number of Italian aviation facilities, and *Flep* 10 settled into the huge airship hangar in Casarsa, about 35 km (22 miles) from Udine. Under the sign 'Montage' (assembly), work is almost complete on D III 153.141, Lloyd C V 46.63 and an unidentified Brandenburg C I, while in the background other aeroplanes await their turn near the crates that will transport them to the frontline. 153.141 was used in the spring and summer of 1918 by Zgf Franz Rudorfer of *Flik* 51/J, who claimed five confirmed victories with this machine *(Koloman Mayrhofer)*

resources and poisoned by its political and social contradictions. Like exhausted boxers in their corners, the rivals got their breath back during the winter of 1917-18, waiting for the spring. The Italian air service used this pause to strengthen its units and train its airmen in the new fighting tactics learnt so expensively in the recent defeat. Although the Austro-Hungarians were strengthened by the arrival of new units from the Russian Front, they lost the German aviation units, which were recalled to the Western Front.

The situation along this front is well described in a highly classified bulletin released by the Italian intelligence service, which summarised the conditions of Austro-Hungarian aviation from November 1917 through to May 1918. Considering data collected from several sources, ranging from analysis of the air activity to interrogation of captured airmen, the paper made the following stark assessment;

'Although all Austro-Hungarian units in full efficiency have spent a long time on the Italian Front, and have been joined by units stationed on the former Russian-Rumanian Front, especially from April, the general scarcity of pilots and engines, and the constant losses due to several causes, but especially to the inexperience of the flight personnel, makes the efficiency of Austro-Hungarian aviation on the Italian Front far inferior to the number of the units placed there.'

The lack of raw materials available to the Hapsburg Empire increased in significance, and in January 1918 came the first strikes caused by chronic food shortages. Incessant nationalistic turmoil also shook the countries of the old Empire. Within a few short months the civilian population and the armed forces would suffer true famine, causing industrial production to decrease both in quantity and quality. The same paper produced by the intelligence arm of the Italian 8th Army again hit the mark with the following appraisal of the situation facing the fighting forces of the Austro-Hungarian Empire;

'It is doubtful whether the number of companies could increase, and this stasis could endure for some time, while the lack of engines, and more importantly the scarcity of personnel, could render difficult not only the formation of new units, but also the activation of those yet formed but already worn out on the Russian Front and subject to continuous losses on the Italian one.'

The accuracy of this evaluation is reflected in the tone of the reports filed by Austro-Hungarian aviation units at this time. These were, in effect, an anthology of sad complaints about the lack of everything, from instruments to bracing wires and even paint, while troubles with the quality of petrol were increasing. Aeroplanes lost were not replaced, and those damaged were not repaired. In addition, training was delayed and the quality of the airmen, especially fighter pilots, decreased, in spite of the establishment of a special *Jagdfliegerschule* (Fighter Aircraft School) in Campoformido, as voiced in a report written by Hptm Stohanzl in June 1918.

Later in the war there were *Flik* that existed only nominally, having neither pilots nor aeroplanes.

On 15 June 1918 the Austro-Hungarian army played its last card when it launched its final offensive, supported by the *LFT*. The campaign, however, ended in defeat, with the Italians also gaining air superiority. The latter proved to be one of the key factors in the Italian victory on the ground.

On the first day of the offensive, the *LFT's* order of battle was as follows (the list of aeroplanes is not complete);

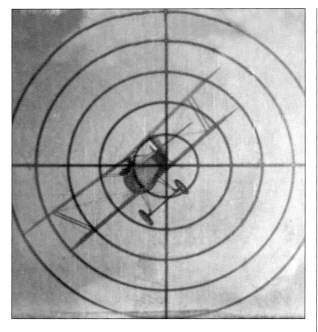

**Hitting the bullseye! A Hanriot HD 1 is framed in the cross-hairs of the gunsight. Although this image was taken by a Hythe gun camera during a mock dogfight in the Italian Fighter School, the photograph well portrays the point-blank range at which World War 1 aerial combats took place** *(Aeronautica Militare Italiana)*

**A line-up of *Flik* 61/J fighters on Motta di Livenza airfield in early 1918. Albatros D III 153.32 at left sports the red wheel discs and slanted stripe on the tail that identified the unit, but retains the white-outlined red band of its former user, *Flik* 19/D, on its fuselage. Behind Aviatik D I 138.17 is D III 53.61, which had previously served with *Flik* 32/D** *(Matjaz Ravbar)*

Pilots of *Flik* 55/J enjoy a bottle of sparkling wine whilst listening to a gramophone record in the early spring sun at Pergine. They are, from left to right, Zgf Alois Lehman, Zgf Alexander Kasza (probably), Kpl Franz Lahner, Kpl Gottlieb Munczar and Fw Alfons Behounek (probably). This house still exists in this form, although only one of the trees remains *(Bohumir Kudlicka)*

***Heeresgruppenkommando*** Feldmarschall Svetozar Boroevic von Boina

***Subordination***

| Unit | Airfield | Commanding Officer | Aeroplanes |
|------|----------|--------------------|-----------|
| *Fliegergruppe G* | | | |
| *Flik* 101/G | Pordenone | *Rittmeister* Max Hesse | Brandenburg C I |
| *Flik* 102/G | Aviano | Oblt Rudolf Weber | Brandenburg C I, Phönix C I |
| *Flik* 103/G | Aviano | Oblt Karl Weigel von Nagikosztolany | Brandenburg C I |
| *Flik* 104/G | Aviano | Oblt Robert Ratzer | No aircraft |
| *Flik* 105/G | Aviano | Oblt Albert Hafergut | Brandenburg C I, Gotha G IV |
| *K u K Isonzoarmee* | | | |
| *Flik* 5/F | Mansuè | Hptm Johann Wierzejski | Brandenburg C I, Aviatik C I |
| *Flik* 12/B | Cleris | Hptm Benno Weber | Phönix C I |
| *Flik* 19/D | Ghirano | Hptm Johann Polivka | Brandenburg C I, Phönix C I |
| *Flik* 22/D | Corbelone | Oblt Wilhelm Ritter von Pichs | Brandenburg C I, Aviatik C I |
| *Flik* 32/D | Mansuè | Hptm Richard Hübner | Brandenburg C I |
| *Flik* 34/D | Corbelone | Oblt Erwin Hauptmann | Brandenburg C I, Phönix C I |
| *Flik* 35/D | Motta di Livenza | Oblt Hugo Mohelsky | Brandenburg C I |
| *Flik* 37/P | S Lorenzo | Hptm Franz Perstinger | Phönix D I |
| *Flik* 41/J | Portobuffolè | Hptm Godwin Brumowski | Albatros D III, Brandenburg C I |
| *Flik* 43/J | Portobuffolè | Hptm Kornelius Kiraly | Phönix D I |
| *Flik* 44/D | Pramaggiore | Hptm Alexander Hangay | Brandenburg C I |
| *Flik* 46/P | Cinto Caomaggiore | Oblt Alexander Weitenschütz | Aviatik C I |

| *Flik* 49/D | Navole | Oblt Georg Altadonna (Temporary) | Brandenburg C I, Aviatik C I |
|---|---|---|---|
| *Flik* 50/D | S Martino | Hptm Cornel Haqué | Brandenburg C I |
| *Flik* 51/J | Ghirano | Hptm Benno Fiala Ritter von Fernbrugg | Albatros D III |
| *Flik* 58/D | Ghirano | Hptm Karl Freiherr von Holtz | UFAG C I, Phönix C I, Aviatik C I |
| *Flik* 61/J | Motta di Livenza | Hptm Ludwig Hautzmayer | Albatros D III |
| *Flik* 62/D | S Martino | Hptm Ernst von Szalay | Brandenburg C I |
| *Flik* 63/J | Motta di Livenza | Oblt Rupert Terk | No aircraft |
| *Flik* 69/S | Gaiarine | Oblt Belisar Suput | Brandenburg C I |
| *Flik* 71/D | Giai | Oblt Ludwig Szabo (Temporary) | Brandenburg C I |

### K u K 6. Armee

| *Flik* 2/D | S Pietro in Campo | Oblt Fritz Losert | Brandenburg C I, Albatros D III |
|---|---|---|---|
| *Flik* 4/D | Gaiarine | Oblt Oskar Futter | Brandenburg C I |
| *Flik* 26/Ds | San Giacomo di Veglia | Hptm Erich Prosch | Brandenburg C I |
| *Flik* 28/D | Godega di San Urbano | Hptm Alexander Hartzer | Brandenburg C I, Phönix C I |
| *Flik* 30/J | S Pietro in Campo | Oblt Hans Fischer | Albatros D III, Phönix D I |
| *Flik* 42/J | Pianzano | Hptm Ladislaus Hary | Albatros D III |
| *Flik* 38/D | San Vendemmiano | Oblt Ladislaus Szendrey | Brandenburg C I |
| *Flik* 56/J | Pianzano | Hptm Robert Hellner | Albatros D III, Aviatik D I |
| *Flik* 68/J | Colle Umberto | Oblt Georg Kenzian Edler von Kenzianshausen | Albatros D III, Phönix D II, Phönix D IIa |
| *Flik* 72/J | S Fior di Sopra | Oblt Josef Hoffmann Ritter von Ostenhof | Aviatik D I |
| *Flik* 74/J | S Fior di Sopra | Oblt Franz Cserich | Aviatik D I |
| *Flik* 40 | Pordenone | Oblt Felix Seigerschmidt | No aircraft |
| *Flik* 47/F | Pianzano | Oblt Walter Cavallar Ritter von Grabensprung | UFAG C I |
| *Flik* 52/D | S Giacomo di Veglia | Hptm Viktor Seebauer | Brandenburg C I |
| *Flik* 57/Rb | Godega di San Urbano | Oblt Adolf Eichberger | Brandenburg C I |
| *Flik* 53/D | S Pietro in Campo | Oblt Johann Schifferer | Brandenburg C I |
| *Flik* 59/D | S Giacomo di Veglia | *Rittmeister* Karl Lukats | Brandenburg C I |
| *Flik* 65/Ds | S Giacomo di Veglia | Hptm Franz Ruprecht Edler von Wahrland | Brandenburg C I |

Although the Empire was dying, Austro-Hungarian airmen continued to fight throughout the summer and even into October, during the final Vittorio Veneto Battle, when all hope was lost. The last available and incomplete data for the *LFT* shows that on 15 October 1918 the order of battle was as follows (again, the list of aeroplanes is not complete);

Oblt Friedrich Navratil claimed a victory with D III 153.198 on 28 June 1918 near Ospedaletto, while StFw Otto Förster scored two confirmed successes while flying 153.200 on 16 July. These were shared with Navratil (flying 253.06 that day) and other *Flik* 3/J pilots. Albatros 153.198 had previously served in *Flik* 17 and *Flik* 27 *(Jiri Rajlich)*

*Heeresgruppenkommando* Feldmarschall Svetozar Boroevic von Boina
*Subordination*

| Unit | Airfield | Commanding Officer | Aeroplane/s |
|---|---|---|---|
| *Grossflugzeuggeschwader* | | | |
| *Flik* 101/G | Pordenone | Oblt Robert Koderle | ? |
| *Flik* 102/G | Aviano | Oblt Rudolf Weber | ? |
| *Flik* 103/G | Aviano | Oblt Rudolf Breier | ? |
| *Flik* 104/G | Aviano | Oblt Robert Ratzer | No aircraft |
| *Flik* 105/G | Aviano | Hptm Franz Schorn | ? |
| *Feldfliegerschule* | Campoformido | Hptm Karl Stohanzl | ? |
| *K u K Isonzoarmee* | | | |
| *Flik* 5/S | Motta di Livenza | Hptm Johann Wierzejski | No aircraft |
| *Flik* 12/Rb | Cleris | Hptm Max Perini | 2 Phönix C Is, 3 Phönix D Is |
| *Flik* 19/K | Ghirano | Hptm Johann Polivka | 1 Brandenburg C I, 5 UFAG C Is |
| *Flik* 22/K | Corbolone | Hptm Emil Kruk | 1 Brandenburg C I, 2 UFAG C Is |
| *Flik* 32/S | Mansuè | Hptm Ernst Ritter von Pfiffer | No aircraft |
| *Flik* 35/K | Motto di Livenza | Hptm Josef Smetana | 3 Brandenburg C Is, 1 UFAG C I |
| *Flik* 37/P | S Lorenzo | Hptm Arthur Kollitsch | 1 Brandenburg C I, 2 Phönix D Is, 4 Aviatik D Is, 2 Albatros D IIIs |
| *Flik* 41/J | Portobuffolè | Oblt Emanuel Streicher | ? |
| *Flik* 43/J | Fossabiuba | Oblt August Domes | ? |
| *Flik* 44/K | Pramaggiore | Hptm Heinrich Schartner | 2 Brandenburg C Is, 1 UFAG C I |
| *Flik* 46/P | Cinto Caomaggiore | Oblt Karl Wrbetzky | 3 Albatros D IIIs, 2 Aviatik D Is, 2 Phönix D Is |
| *Flik* 49/S | Navole | Hptm Stefan Horvath | ? |
| *Flik* 50/S | S Martino | Hptm Cornel Haqué | No aircraft |
| *Flik* 51/J | Ghirano | Ltn Franz Rusorfer | |
| *Flik* 58/F | Beano | Oblt Gustav Rubritius | 1 UFAG C I, 3 Phönix C Is, 1 Aviatik C I |
| *Flik* 61/J | Motta di Livenza | Hptm Ludwig Hautzmayer | ? |
| *Flik* 62/K | S Martino | Hptm Ernst von Szalay | 1 Phönix C I, 1 UFAG C I |
| *Flik* 63/J | Portobuffolè | Oblt Fritz Huber | ? |
| *Flik* 69/S | Gaiarine | Oblt Belisar Suput | 8 Brandenburg C Is, 1 Albatros D III, |
| *Flik* 71/S | Giai | Oblt Karl Neuhüttler (Temporary) | 17 Brandenburg C Is |

***K u K 6. Armee***

| | | | |
|---|---|---|---|
| *Flik* 4/P | Gaiarine | Oblt Oskar Futter | 4 UFAG C Is |
| *Flik* 26/S | Cordenons | Oblt Josef Pospisil | 5 Brandenburg C Is |
| *Flik* 28/K | Godega di San Urbano | Hptm Alexander Hartzer | 4 UFAG C Is |
| *Flik* 38/S | Tovena | Oblt Adolf Eichberger | No aircraft |
| *Flik* 40/P | S Giacomo di Veglia | Oblt Matthäus Schwarz | 6 Aviatik D Is, 1 Phönix D I, 1 Albatros D III |
| *Flik* 42/J | Pianzano | Oblt Georg Kenzian von Kenzianhausen | ? |
| *Flik* 47/F | Cordenons | Oblt Walter Cavallar Ritter von Grabensprung | 8 Brandenburg C Is |
| *Flik* 52/K | Tovena | Hptm Viktor Seebauer | 1 Brandenburg C I, 4 UFAG C Is |
| *Flik* 56/J | Pianzano | Hptm Eugen Oancea | ? |
| *Flik* 57/Rb | S Giacomo di Veglia | Oblt Ladislaus Szendrey | 2 Brandenburg C Is |
| *Flik* 59/S | Cordenons | *Rittmeister* Karl Lukats | No aircraft |
| *Flik* 65/S | Cordenons | Hptm Franz Ruprecht Edler von Wahrland | 4 Brandenburg C Is |
| *Flik* 68/J | Godega di San Urbano | Oblt Julis Koczor (Temporary) | ? |
| *Flik* 72/J | S Fior di Sopra | Oblt Josef Hoffmann Ritter von Ostenhof | No aircraft |
| *Flik* 74/J | S Fior di Sopra | Oblt Roman Schmidt | ? |
| *Flik* 70/P | S Giacomo di Veglia | Hptm Ernst Zimmermann | 4 Aviatik D Is |

***Armeegruppe* Belluno**

| | | | |
|---|---|---|---|
| *Flik* 2/K | Feltre | Oblt Fritz Losert | 5 Brandenburg C Is |
| *Flik* 8/S | S Pietro in Campo | Hptm Oskar Lestin | 3 Brandenburg C Is |
| *Flik* 11/F | S Pietro in Campo | Hptm Oskar Schmoczer von Meczenzef | 3 Brandenburg C Is, 2 UFAG C Is, 1 Phönix C I |
| *Flik* 14/J | Santa Giustina | Oblt Rudolf Stanger | ? |
| *Flik* 16/K | Feltre | Hptm Erwin Schwarzböck | 1 Brandenburg C I, 2 UFAG C Is |
| *Flik* 30/J | Santa Giustina | Oblt Hans Fische | ? |
| *Flik* 39/P | S Pietro in Campo | Oblt Karl Jasny | 1 UFAG C I, 8 Phönix D Is |
| *Flik* 53/S | S Pietro in Campo | Oblt Johann Schifferer | 2 Brandenburg C Is, 2 UFAG C Is |
| *Flik* 60/J | Santa Giustina | Oblt Karl Tilscher | ? |
| *Flik* 66/K | Feltre | Hptm Eugen Macher | 3 Brandenburg C Is, 1 UFAG C I |

***Heeresgruppe GO Erzherhog Joseph***
***K u K 11. Armee***

| | | | |
|---|---|---|---|
| *Flik* 9/J | Ospedaletto | Oblt Stefan Stec | ? |
| *Flik* 15/F | Levico | Oblt Adalbert Kuncze | 1 Brandenburg C I, 5 UFAG C Is |
| *Flik* 20/J | Egna | Oblt Josef Bratmann | ? |
| *Flik* 21/K | Pergine | Hptm Oskar Fekete | 8 Aviatik C Is |
| *Flik* 24/K | Pergine | Hptm Hugo Schwab | 2 Brandenburg C Is, 8 UFAG C Is |
| *Flik* 31/P | Levico | Oblt Fritz Wöde | 2 Brandenburg C Is, 11 Aviatik D Is |
| *Flik* 36/K | Novaledo | Oblt Josef Brunner | 6 Brandenburg C Is, 3 UFAG C Is |
| *Flik* 45/S | Ospedaletto | Oblt Eduard Lewak | ? |
| *Flik* 48/S | Pergine | Oblt Alfons Marincovich | 8 Brandenburg C Is |

| | | | |
|---|---|---|---|
| *Flik* 55/J | Pergine | Oblt Eduard Ritter vob Hebra | ? |
| **K u K 10. Armee** | | | |
| *Flik* 3/J | Romagnano | Oblt Friedrich Navratil | ? |
| *Flik* 7/G | Gardolo | Oblt Max Schossleitner (Temporary) | ? |
| *Flik* 10/P | Gardolo | Oblt Otto Wehofer | ? |
| *Flik* 17/K | Gardolo | Hptm Aurel Schiavon | ? |
| *Flik* 23/K | Gardolo | Oblt Maximilian Bondy | ? |
| *Flik* 27/F | Gardolo | Hptm Franz Smicka | ? |
| *Flik* 54/K | Campo Maggiore | Hptm Karl Schiller | ? |
| *Flik* 73/K | Croviana | Oblt Rudolf Lassmann | ? |

During the war Italy built 12,382 aeroplanes, Great Britain 54,783, France 52,146 and Germany 47,931, while the *LFT* accepted only 4768 aircraft. The Austro-Hungarian situation was well described in the *Österreichisch-Ungarischen Generalstabswerkes 1914-1918,* although the numbers quoted do not accord with recent studies;

'The seven aircraft industries and six engine factories working in Austria-Hungary for aviation were able to build 1740 aeroplanes and 1230 engines in 1917, and 2378 aircraft and 1750 engines in 1918. In this way the industry had broadly fulfilled the expectations of 1916. But this production was not even able to reach the goal of 68 *Flik* and 3 *Grosskampfgeschwader* by the end of 1917, because the attrition rate of aircraft was high. You could count on an aircraft having an average life of only four months, so production at the turn of the years 1917/1918 could only keep the number of operational aircraft at 450-500 units. Because there could be no further increase in production, and because problems with the supply of materials put the productivity temporarily

The metal kite balloon emblem on the collar of Zgf Karl Teichmann's tunic was the badge of the *LFT*. On his chest is pinned the Silver Bravery Medal 2nd Class. He later received the 1st Class medal and the Golden Bravery Medal, ending the war with five confirmed victories *(Greg VanWyngarden)*

An assortment of personal insignia on the Albatros D IIIs of *Flik* 3/J on Romagnano airfield in the summer of 1918. These aircraft are, from left to right, 153.173 with a red-and-white chessboard (Ltn Stanislav Maria Tomicki von Tomice), 153.225 with a lightning flash, 253.06 with a heart pierced by an arrow (Oblt Friedrich Navratil), 153.227 with a three-pointed star, 153.244 (probably) with a swastika and 153.234 with a horizontal 'S' (Oblt Stefan Stec). Only Navratil's machine features the new straight-armed national insignia *(Jiri Rajlich)*

Oblt August Selinger of *Flik* 42/J poses in front of Albatros D III 153.202, which has been adorned with the 'Punto Nero' (Black Dot) insignia. He was forced to land this aeroplane on Pianzano airfield on 25 June 1918 after a fight over the Montello, thus becoming a probable victim of Hanriots from *76ª Squadriglia* piloted by Tenenti Silvio Scaroni and Giulio Lega and Sergente Romolo Ticconi, who had 26, 5 and 6 victories, respectively, by war's end. Selinger escaped unhurt, but was shot down again and killed on 28 August near Portobuffolè *(Greg VanWyngarden)*

*Flik* 63/J marked its aeroplanes with black-and-white stripes on the tail and with sectors of the same colours on the wheel discs. In addition to the unit insignia, D III 153.238 has an arrow hitting a bullseye on its fuselage side. Fw Johann Nemeth flew this aeroplane from Portobuffolè airfield during the last summer of the war *(Greg VanWyngarden)*

On 23 September 1918 the *LFT's* already critical situation in respect to the number of aircraft it could field was made even worse by a hurricane of unusual violence that wrought havoc on the Venetian plain, destroying or damaging many aeroplanes of all types. Albatros D III 253.32, which had been flown by Zgf Rudolf Nemetz in August, was almost overturned, revealing that the new crosses were painted beside the old ones, which were obliterated by dark paint. The *Flik* 63/J markings described previously are clearly visible on the rear section of the fighter's fuselage, as well as on the wheel discs *(Jiri Rajlich)*

In the final days of the war, Italian reconnaissance aeroplanes constantly overflew enemy airfields to check on the disposition of *LFT* aircraft. This photograph of Portobuffolè airfield was taken on 27 October by an SVA of *87ª Squadriglia*. The Italian intelligence officers noted significant details in black ink, and number '4' marks a typical polygonal Austro-Hungarian fabric hangar (*Aeronautica Militare Italiana*)

attained at risk, a further expansion of the Austro-Hungarian air force in order to reach even the approximate size of the opposing force was absolutely out of the question.

'In the meantime the Supreme Command (*AOK*) had decided on a further increase to 1000 pilots and 100 *Fliegerkompagnien*, but these figures could not be reached at all. By the autumn of 1918 there were 72 *Fliegerkompagnien*, but even this slight increase did not appear to achieve any strengthening of the force, owing to the incompleteness of all *Fliegerkompagnien*.

'So the Austro-Hungarian airmen based on the Southwest Front had to face an increasingly numerically superior enemy who also had better machines. Nonetheless, they fought thousands of times in unequal combats and accomplished admirable things, thus deserving the highest praise.'

Forlorn and plundered, five Albatros D IIIs and a Phönix fighter await their fate while cold Italian soldiers walk across a foggy Bressanone airfield, in the South Tyrol, on the first day of peace. The captured aeroplanes were gathered by the new owners on airfields in the old war zone, but they were probably deemed to be of no interest because there is no official documentation to indicate that they were test-flown post-war. Conversely, the Italian air force intensively flew captured German aeroplanes, and they remained in service for many years, sometimes still carrying wartime insignia (*Aeronautica Militare Italiana*)

# RUSSIAN, RUMANIAN AND ALBANIAN FRONTS

The first Albatros D IIs arrived on the Eastern Front in the summer of 1917, where they were soon joined by the D III. The aeroplanes were used in Galicia by *Flik* 3, 14, 20, 22, 25 and 37, and in Bukovina by *Flik* 7 and 26. The first victory for the new fighter in this theatre of operations was achieved on 26 June by *Flik* 25 pilot Kpl Rudolf Blass, who, flying Albatros D II 53.11, claimed a Russian Voisin near Koniuchy for his first confirmed success.

On 20 July, while escorting Brandenburg C I 64.35 of *Flik* 27, Oblt Otto Jäger, flying D III 53.45, forced an aircraft described as a 'Russian two-seater with a red-white cockade on the fuselage' to crash-land near Wibudow (now Vybudiv in the Ukraine). This was his first victory as a pilot and his sixth in total, as he had achieved the first five as an observer with *Flik* 10. For this victory Jäger was presented with the *Silberne Militärverdienstmedaille mit Schwerten* (Silver Military Merit Medal with Swords). Born in West Bohemia on 6 April 1890, Jäger came to aviation after being wounded three times while serving with the infantry. Deemed unfit for further service as a soldier, he transferred to the *LFT* instead.

Two months after Jäger's success, a victory was claimed by 25-year-old Hungarian hussar Oblt Rudolf Szepessy-Sokoll von Negies et Reno, who was serving with *Flik* 3. Born into a family with a military tradition (his great-grandfather held the prestigious *Militär-Maria-Theresiaorden* (Military Order Of Maria Theresa)), he too had initially fought on the ground during the early stages of World War 1. Awarded the *Silberne Tapferkeitsmedaillen 1. Klasse* (Silver Bravery Medals 1st Class) and the Bronze Military Merit Medal during this period, Szepessy-Sokoll had subsequently been accepted into Army Aviation and had flown as an observer on the Italian Front with *Flik* 17. One of his early missions was the 14 February 1916 air raid on Milan from Gardolo, in South Tyrol, flying with pilot Zgf Philipp Possl in Lohner B VII 17.36. On this occasion Austrian-Hungarian sources claim the shooting

On a snowy Russian airfield a mechanic holds the tail of Albatros D II 53.12 on the trestle to prevent the aeroplane flipping over during an engine test. As usual in cold conditions, the cowling is fitted to keep the engine warm. There is a rack for flare cartridges alongside the cockpit. This machine was used by *Flik* 20 in Galicia in June 1917 *(Boris Ciglic)*

An unidentified senior officer is seen here alongside 53.20, the first Albatros D III to arrive in Bukovina. It was flown from here by Zgf Karl Semmelrock in July and August 1917. With this aeroplane Oblt Hans Fischer of *Kampfstaffel Galanesti* claimed a fighter near Mihaleni on 3 October. However, 11 days later, Fw Johann Obesio was shot down in it by Praporshchik Grigory Eduardovich Suk of the Imperial Russian Air Service during a dogfight southeast of Radauti, in Rumania *(Greg VanWyngarden)*

down of an Italian Caudron that does not match any known loss.

After pilot training, Szepessy-Sokoll returned to the Russian Front and was assigned to *Flik* 27, later being attached to *Flik* 3 as a fighter pilot. On 20 September he clashed with an aeroplane described as a 'Nieuport two-seater' near Kadlubisko, west of Boratin, and shot it down in flames about two or three kilometres (one to two miles) within the Russian lines. This victory was reported in the *Heerebericht* one month later. The Nieuport's crew, Mladshiy Unter-ofitser Ovseiko and Porutschik Nikolai Ivanovic Gogulinski, did not survive the crash.

Szepessy-Sokoll's next victory (his third) was also cited in the Heerebericht. On 4 October he attacked a Russian observation balloon near Iwanczony at low altitude and set it ablaze. On this occasion his Albatros D III, 53.45, returned to its airfield with evidence of hits by several bullets from anti-aircraft machine guns.

The pilots of *Flik* 37 judged the Albatros D II slow, and complained that due to its poor rate of climb they could not intercept the Russian aeroplanes that seldom crossed the lines. This restricted pilots to performing mostly escort duties for photo-reconnaissance aircraft. Nevertheless, the D II proved to be a useful training tool when it came to converting two-seater pilots onto single-seat fighters.

Although there were no specialised *Flik* committed to this theatre, Albatros series 53.2 and 153 aircraft were employed on the Russian–Rumanian Front in makeshift fighter units. For example, in July 1917 the *Fliegerdetachement Nikitsch* (Aviation Detachment Nikitsch) was established, named after its commanding officer, Hptm Karl Nikitsch, and assigned to *Flik* 31 in the 1st Army sector in Transylvania. Nikitsch obtained his first victory flying the new fighter on 19 July. He was patrolling the front in Albatros D III 53.24 when he spotted a Farman

Accepted by the *LFT* in August 1917, Albatros D III 153.24 saw service on the Eastern Front with *Kampfstaffel Harja*. Later, when it was with *Kampfstaffel Galanesti*, Zgf Wilhelm Haring was flying it when he claimed a two-seater on 7 November 1917. This photograph was taken at Czernowitz airfield, in Bukovina, during the spring of 1918 *(Greg VanWyngarden)*

two-seater and attacked it. After he had fired about 150 rounds of 8 mm ammunition at point-blank range the Farman dived, crashing near Fitionesti.

On 23 July Nikitsch achieved his second victory while escorting a reconnaissance aircraft of *Flik* 29. After taking off from Focsani airfield in D III 53.41, he attacked two Farman biplanes over Iresti, firing several bursts, but a SPAD fighter bounced him from the rear. Nikitsch was able to reverse the position and fired 50 bullets, whereupon the SPAD went into a vertical dive and crashed near Zabrau.

*Fliegerdetachement Nikitsch* had seven confirmed victories during September. The following month the unit was reorganised and its name changed to *Fliegerdetachement Harja,* after the airfield near Kézdivásárhely, or *Jagdstaffel Oberleutnant Terk*, after the name of its new commanding officer, Rupert Terk. Two more victories were added before the end of 1917, on 28 October and on 7 November.

From September 1917 one more provisional unit saw action over Bukovina, in the operational area of the 7th Army, attached to *Flik* 40/D. This unit, which claimed two victories before the ceasefire, was commanded by Prague-born officer Oblt Hans Fischer and based on Galanesti airfield, thus being named *Kampfstaffel Galanesti*.

The Armistice took effect on 18 December 1917, and some of the pilots who flew Albatros fighters on the Eastern Front started new tours of duty in the Italian theatre, which offered them further opportunities to gain victories, or to die.

## ALBANIAN FRONT

The Oeffag fighters also faced the Italian air force on the Albanian front, where D IIIs 53.28 and 53.30 arrived in June 1917 and were assigned to *Flik* 6 at Tirana airfield. On 4 February 1918 Zgf Michael Schwach, flying 53.28, engaged with fighters of *85ª Squadriglia* and claimed a Nieuport destroyed, but there is no trace of this machine among the Italian losses.

Albatros 53.28 had a long operational career that lasted until 7 July 1918, when it was burnt by the ground personnel of the *Flik* to prevent its capture by Italian cavalry as they overran Fjeri airfield. On that occasion *Flik* 6 and 64 also lost two Aviatik D Is, two Brandenburg C Is and a Fokker D II used as trainer, plus 62 men.

Albatros 53.30 was flown by several pilots, including, in the spring of 1918, the second most successful ace of the *LFT*, Offz Stv Julius Arigi. He had left the front in Italy in January 1918 owing to illness and subsequently arrived in Albania in April of that year for a second tour of duty in this theatre. Arigi obtained his final victories in Albania during the last summer of the war, after which he was posted to Hennesdorf to work as a test pilot for the WKF Factory.

Fw Julius Arigi flew his first tour of duty in the Balkans, and obtained his first victory with *Flik* 6 in Albania, before being moved to the Italian Front. He returned to this unit in April 1918. In this photograph only two medals are pinned over the left breast pocket of his tunic, but by the end of the war Arigi was the most decorated NCO in the whole army *(Jiri Rajlich)*

Albatros D III 53.30 of *Flik* 6 in Albania, probably on Tirana airfield, with Arigi in the cockpit. Delivered in June 1917, this aeroplane was still operational in the spring of the following year, in spite of a crash on 26 August 1917. During the fighter's repair the Schwarzlose machine gun on the upper wing was replaced by a synchronised weapon in the nose *(Jiri Rajlich)*

# THE ITALIAN FRONT

**U**p to the beginning of 1917 the *Flik* were not specialised, undertaking all aerial tasks from reconnaissance to artillery spotting and fighter and escort missions. In theory they had six two-seaters ready for use and two more in the stores of the *Fliegerersatzpark* (*Flep* – aviation replacement park), and a staff comprising a commanding officer, a *Chefpilot* officer to test new aeroplanes, seven non-commissioned officer pilots and eight observer officers. The ground personnel consisted of a technical officer and 163 men. However, a shortage of men, machines and spare parts rarely allowed this status to be achieved, and the situation worsened with the continuation of the war.

In the early months of 1917 the *LFT* formed its first pure fighter units on the Isonzo Front, creating *Flik* 41 and 42 with KDs, while two or three single-seaters were also given to other units for escort and defence tasks. In May 1917 four Albatros – 53.01, 53.02, 53.04 and 53.09 – were sent to Wiener Neustadt airfield and assigned to *Flek* 6 (*Fliegerersatzkompagnie* – aviation replacement company) to introduce the pilots to the new aeroplanes.

These aircraft had arrived just in the nick of time as the Italians were planning an offensive on the Asiago Plateau. Pressure exerted by the Italian aviation units on the Austro-Hungarian *Flik* on the South Tyrolean Front forced the *LFT* to move the Albatros fighters to this area of operation. 53.01, 53.02 and 53.09 duly left *Flek* 6 for Pergine, an airfield in a narrow valley about ten kilometres (six miles) from Trento that was under the control of the 11th Army. There, the Albatros joined the three KDs of *Flik* 21, 24 and 48 to form a provisional fighter unit, the *Alarm Bereitschaft Pergine* (Alarm Detachment Pergine) or *Jagdstaffel Oberleutnant Elssler*, named after its commanding officer, Oblt Wilhelm Elssler. Post-war, the latter (who was a descendant of a famous Austrian ballerina)

In May 1917 Albatros D II 53.01 was sent to *Flek* 6 in Wiener Neustadt to be used to train pilots on the new type, after which it was transferred to Pergine airfield at the front. On 26 June FR Wilhelm Elssler took off in this aircraft to protect the airfield during a visit of the *Kaiser*, and clashed over Val d'Assa with an enemy fighter, possibly the Nieuport flown by the Italian ace Tenente Fulco Ruffo di Calabria. The Albatros was damaged and forced to land, turning over near Levico. Elssler was unhurt, but 53.01 was written off the following month

would become the pilot of the future chancellor Engelbert Dollfuss when he was Minister for Forestry and Agriculture.

At 1715 hrs on 10 June the guns started a heavy shelling of the Austro-Hungarian lines, opening what would become known as the Ortigara Battle. The Italian troops then screamed their battle cry 'Savoia!' and left their trenches for the first attack. This ultimately proved to be yet another bloodbath, having cost the Italians some 23,000 casualties without result by the time it ended on 29 June – a similar outcome to the attacks along the Isonzo River.

Although bad weather hampered aviation activity during the Ortigara Battle, the new Albatros fighter still managed to achieve its first victory. In the early afternoon of the first day of the offensive, Fw Julius Kowalczik of *Flik* 24, flying Albatros D II 53.02, shot down a Caproni bomber of *5ª Squadriglia* that had taken off from Tombetta di Verona airfield with two other two aircraft at 1350 hrs to attack hutments in Val Galmarara and Val Portule. The crew of Ca.2368 (pilots Tenente Emilio Lodesani and Tenente Max Arici, observer Tenente Federico Caneva and gunner Maresciallo Romeo Betteghella) all died when the bomber crashed in flames at Val Portule. Buried with military honours by the Austro-Hungarian troops, the crew also received the *Medaglia d'Argento al Valor Militare* from the command of the *I Armata* (Army) on 17 June.

Kowalczik shared this victory with Brandenburg C Is 29.73 of *Flik* 17 (flown by Fw Karl Maurer and observer Ltn Max Schlossleitner) and 129.23 of *Flik* 21 (flown by Fw Richard Schuster and observer Ltn Franz Neuburger).

Kowalczik, born of German parents in 1885 in Märisch Ostrau (now Moravska Ostrava in the Czech Republic), volunteered for the air service in late 1915, obtaining his pilot's certificate on 16 February 1916. After a period with *Flik* 15, he was assigned in May of that year to the newly-established *Flik* 24, a general-purpose unit based in

The first Albatros victory in aerial combat was claimed by Fw Julius Kowalczik of *Alarm Bereitschaft Pergine* on 10 June 1917 over Val Portule, when a Caproni bomber of *2ª Squadriglia* was shot down by D III 53.02. The aeroplane had been sent to the Italian front with the first batch of fighters from *Flep* 6, and it was flown until written off in a takeoff incident in September *(Rudi Höfling)*

In this Austrian photograph a Caproni bomber flies over snowy mountains, probably in the northern sector of the front. Although strongly built, and defended by three machine guns, these aircraft did not usually cross the lines alone. Typically, they would be escorted by fighters, and fly in tight formation to provide a crossfire to deter adversaries *(WAF Archive)*

On Sesana airfield NCO pilots of *Flik* 41/J pose in front of D III 53.15 on 21 June 1917. They are, from left to right, Zgf Josef Nowak, Zgf Hermann Richter, Zgf Ferdinand Jaschek, Fw Karl Kaszaka, Zgf Jaroslav Samek and Zgf Radames Iskra. The triangular Oeffag logo is visible on the aircraft's nose, just above Richter's head *(Rudi Höfling)*

Pergine under the command of Hptm Gustav Studeny. Promoted to zugsführer, Kowalczik gained his first confirmed victory on 14 October 1916 whilst flying with 46-year-old Artillery Staff Oberst Leo Nadherny as observer in Brandenburg C I 61.18.

On that day, in company with Brandenburg C I 61.23, crewed by Zgf Wenzel Schwarz and Oblt Johann Fischer, they spotted an Italian Farman at a lower altitude and attacked it. The Italian observer was seen firing his machine gun at 61.81, but he soon fell to the fire from the second Brandenburg. When the pilot was also hit the Farman side-slipped and crashed not far from Pergine airfield, whereupon the petrol tank burst into flames. The fallen airmen of *31ª Squadriglia*, pilot Sergente Francesco Bobbio and observer Capitano Felice Cantele, were buried in the cemetery at Pergine and the Austro-Hungarian airmen placed a wreath on their graves.

Kowalczik achieved ace status on 19 June when he claimed his fifth, and last, victory of the war. His quarry was a Caudron intercepted near Cima Maora, on the Asiago Plateau, the aeroplane, probably belonging to *50ª Squadriglia*, being on its way back after the bombardment of Val d'Assa. Its pilot, Aspirante Amedeo Mecozzi (a future Italian five-victory ace and a theoretician of close-support aviation between the wars), was able to crash-land near Santorso and escape unhurt with his observer, Sottotenente Giulio Mazzocchini. For the second time the Austro-Hungarian non-commissioned officer received the *Goldene Tapferkeitmedaille* (Gold Bravery Medal) from Kaiser Karl I in person during his visit to Pergine airfield on 26 June.

More Albatros began to arrive in the war zone, and on 30 June there were two D IIs (53.01 and 53.09) and six D IIIs (53.29, 53.33, 53.34, 53.36, 53.39 and 53.44) in Pergine. The new fighter also made its debut on the Isonzo Front with *Flik* 41 and 42 at Sesana airfield. That same day *Flik* 41 had one D II (53.15) and one D III (53.27), while the sister unit was equipped with a single D II (53.13).

The delivery of the new fighters was very necessary. The Italians had just ended their tenth offensive over the Isonzo and, although the conflict on the ground yielded few results for the massive effort and the losses incurred, Italian air superiority was confirmed thanks to the arrival on the front of new units and new aircraft, especially Nieuport 17 and SPAD VII fighters.

The desperate efforts of the *5. Armee* (Army) were honoured by the *Kaiser* naming the force the *Isonzoarmee*, but the situation was critical, as stated in a document quoted by Austrian historian Karl Meindl;

'Throughout the period the enemy's air superiority was felt more and more heavily. The Italians maintained an air barrage with fast and manoeuvrable Nieuport and SPAD aircraft at heights between 1000-5000 m [3300-16,400 ft] all along the *Isonzoarmee* front. They are

always in the majority. Our aircraft can no longer be sent alone on reconnaissance missions. Our two fighter *Flik* are not even able, despite the utmost use of their potential, to escort all the reconnaissance aircraft, so they were used as emergency escort to other reconnaissance aeroplanes.

'The superiority of the Italian single-seat fighter and combat aircraft was supported by an optical signalling system that worked very well. As soon as our aeroplanes reach the front, signal and smoke rockets of different colours are fired, and shortly thereafter several fighter aeroplanes already in patrol over the front sector arrive for the barrage. If to this is added the use of fire and explosive rounds by the enemy fighters, the Italians have the undisputed advantage. This superiority was reflected in increasingly frequent raids behind the Austro-Hungarian lines of bomber squadrons during the day, which severely hampered the movement of any traffic. The new Capronis were far faster and more agile than the older ones, and could only be fought successfully in the air with great difficulty.'

During this period the KD was still in frontline service, and often the two types fought side by side. In spite of its faults the Brandenburg D I could be effective when handled by an expert pilot. These included 21-year-old StFw Josef Kiss, born to a humble family of Hungarian origin in what is now Bratislava. Kiss left school at the outbreak of war to enlist, thus excluding himself from the possibility of becoming an officer according to the strict rules of the Austro-Hungarian Army. He became a pilot after being wounded during infantry service on the Russian Front. Daring and talented in air combats, which he is said to have regarded as a 'dangerous sport', without hating his adversaries, 'Josi' liked to swim with other local boys in the Caldonazzo Lake, where he arrived on a motorcycle. By the time he had become an ace on 14 June 1917 he was already famous, receiving letters and pictures from unknown girls.

On 13 July Kiss, still flying KD 28.37, obtained his sixth victory near Levico when he shared in the forcing down of Italian Savoia Pomilio SP.4530 of *26ª Squadriglia* with Albatros D III 53.33 of Fw Viktor Zimmermann and a Brandenburg C I of *Flik* 17 piloted by Fw Karl Maurer, with Oblt Erich Kühne as observer. The Italian pilot, Tenente Vitale Piga, wrote after his return from captivity;

'During the morning of 13 July 1917 I received the order to perform an orientation reconnaissance and to drop leaflets for the prisoners in the Austrian rear line between Adige and Brenta. With me was Tenente observer Semplicini, who beside dropping the leaflets had also to take a series of photographs.

On 13 July Fw Viktor Zimmerman, flying D III 53.33, shared with Kiss and a Brandenburg C I crew the shooting down of Savoia-Pomilio SP.4530 of *26ª Squadriglia*. Its observer, Tenente Semplicini, was killed during the fight, and his pilot, Tenente Piga, was captured. He subsequently met the Austro-Hungarian ace who had been forced to land nearby owing to engine trouble *(Ivo Michael Forti)*

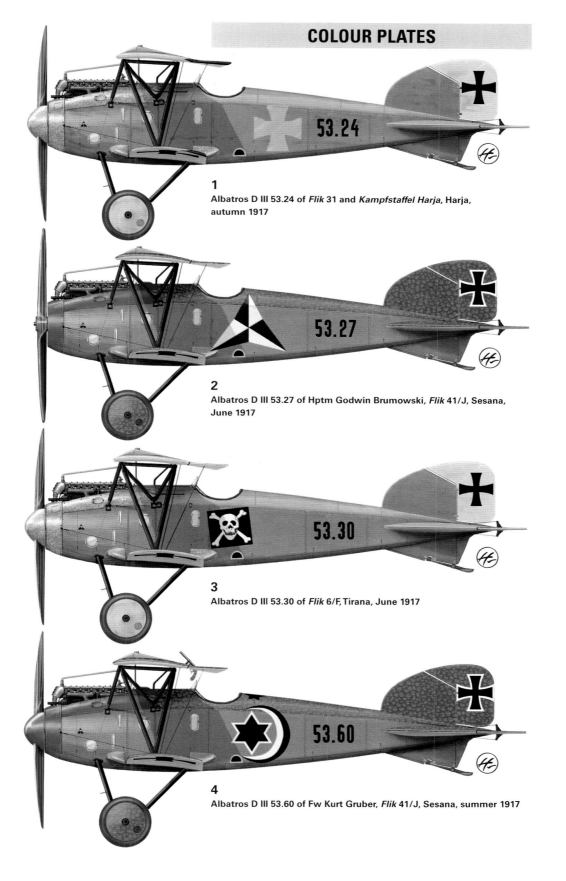

**1**
Albatros D III 53.24 of *Flik* 31 and *Kampfstaffel Harja*, Harja, autumn 1917

**2**
Albatros D III 53.27 of Hptm Godwin Brumowski, *Flik* 41/J, Sesana, June 1917

**3**
Albatros D III 53.30 of *Flik* 6/F, Tirana, June 1917

**4**
Albatros D III 53.60 of Fw Kurt Gruber, *Flik* 41/J, Sesana, summer 1917

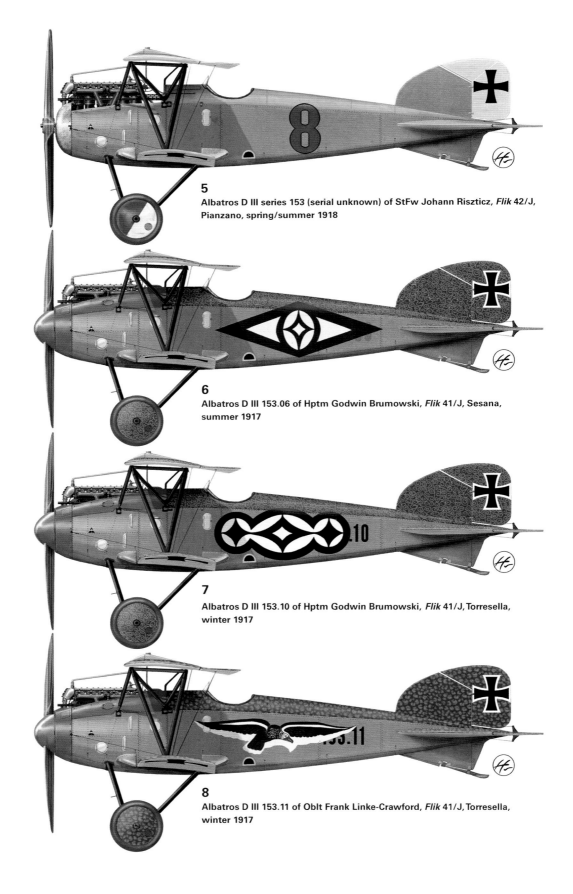

**5**
Albatros D III series 153 (serial unknown) of StFw Johann Riszticz, *Flik* 42/J, Pianzano, spring/summer 1918

**6**
Albatros D III 153.06 of Hptm Godwin Brumowski, *Flik* 41/J, Sesana, summer 1917

**7**
Albatros D III 153.10 of Hptm Godwin Brumowski, *Flik* 41/J, Torresella, winter 1917

**8**
Albatros D III 153.11 of Oblt Frank Linke-Crawford, *Flik* 41/J, Torresella, winter 1917

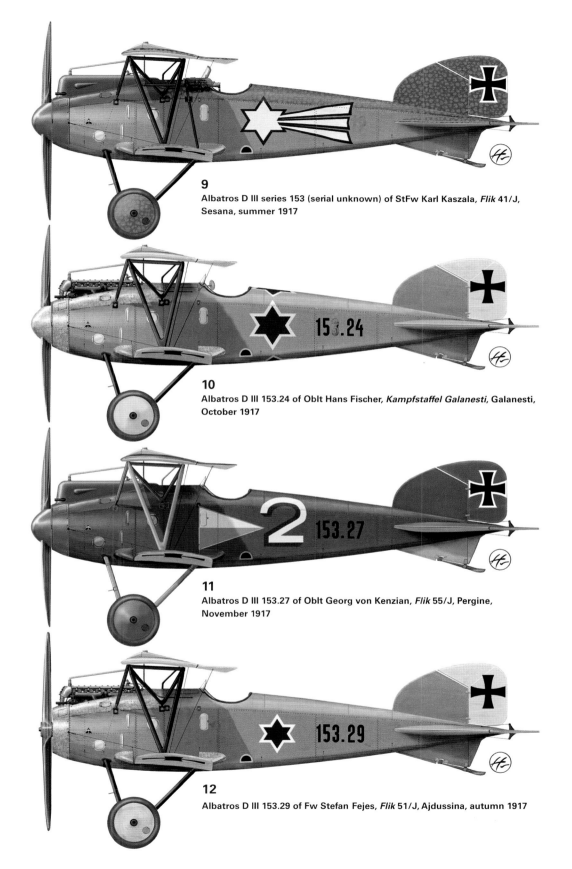

**9**
Albatros D III series 153 (serial unknown) of StFw Karl Kaszala, *Flik* 41/J,
Sesana, summer 1917

**10**
Albatros D III 153.24 of Oblt Hans Fischer, *Kampfstaffel Galanesti*, Galanesti,
October 1917

**11**
Albatros D III 153.27 of Oblt Georg von Kenzian, *Flik* 55/J, Pergine,
November 1917

**12**
Albatros D III 153.29 of Fw Stefan Fejes, *Flik* 51/J, Ajdussina, autumn 1917

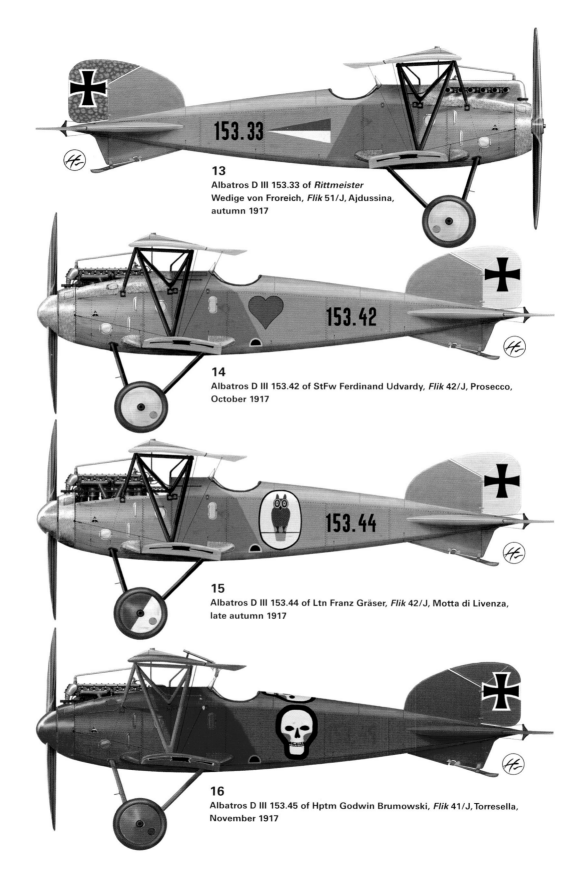

**13**
Albatros D III 153.33 of *Rittmeister*
Wedige von Froreich, *Flik* 51/J, Ajdussina,
autumn 1917

**14**
Albatros D III 153.42 of StFw Ferdinand Udvardy, *Flik* 42/J, Prosecco,
October 1917

**15**
Albatros D III 153.44 of Ltn Franz Gräser, *Flik* 42/J, Motta di Livenza,
late autumn 1917

**16**
Albatros D III 153.45 of Hptm Godwin Brumowski, *Flik* 41/J, Torresella,
November 1917

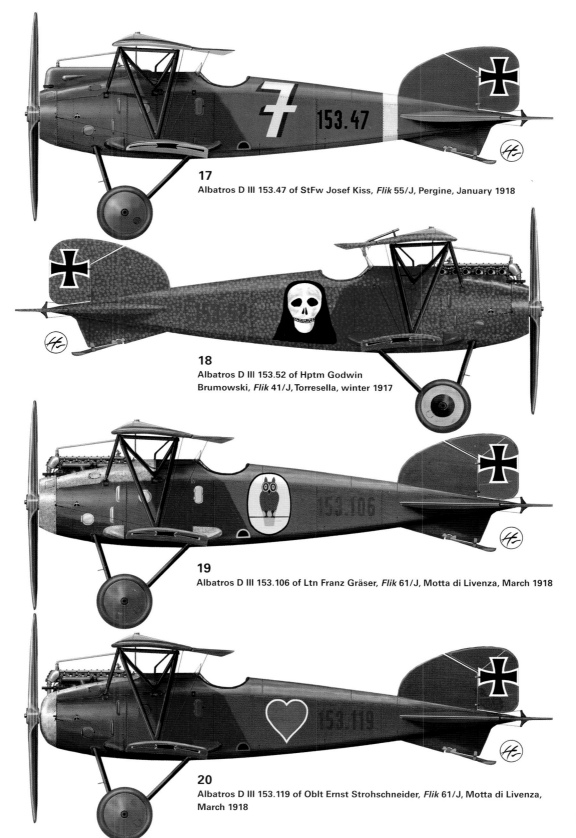

**17**
Albatros D III 153.47 of StFw Josef Kiss, *Flik* 55/J, Pergine, January 1918

**18**
Albatros D III 153.52 of Hptm Godwin
Brumowski, *Flik* 41/J, Torresella, winter 1917

**19**
Albatros D III 153.106 of Ltn Franz Gräser, *Flik* 61/J, Motta di Livenza, March 1918

**20**
Albatros D III 153.119 of Oblt Ernst Strohschneider, *Flik* 61/J, Motta di Livenza,
March 1918

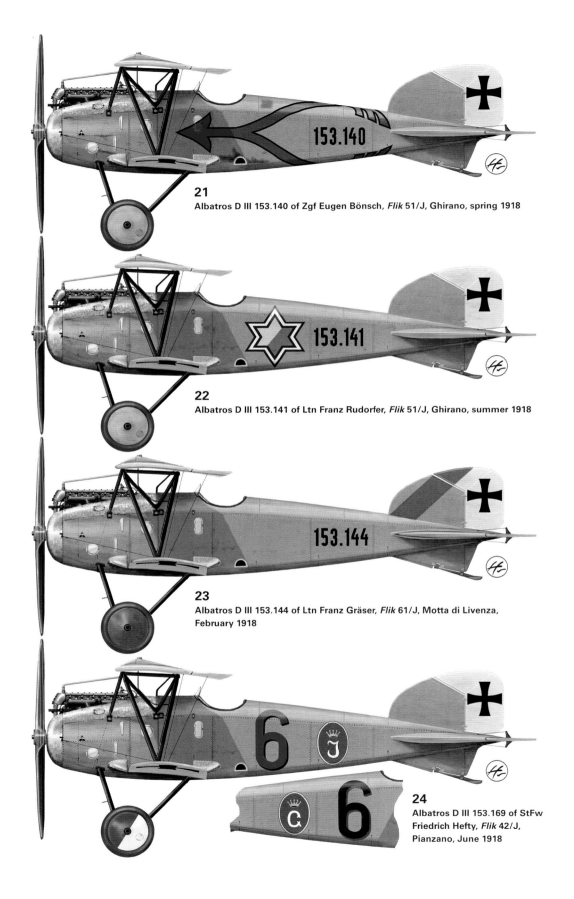

**21**
Albatros D III 153.140 of Zgf Eugen Bönsch, *Flik* 51/J, Ghirano, spring 1918

**22**
Albatros D III 153.141 of Ltn Franz Rudorfer, *Flik* 51/J, Ghirano, summer 1918

**23**
Albatros D III 153.144 of Ltn Franz Gräser, *Flik* 61/J, Motta di Livenza, February 1918

**24**
Albatros D III 153.169 of StFw Friedrich Hefty, *Flik* 42/J, Pianzano, June 1918

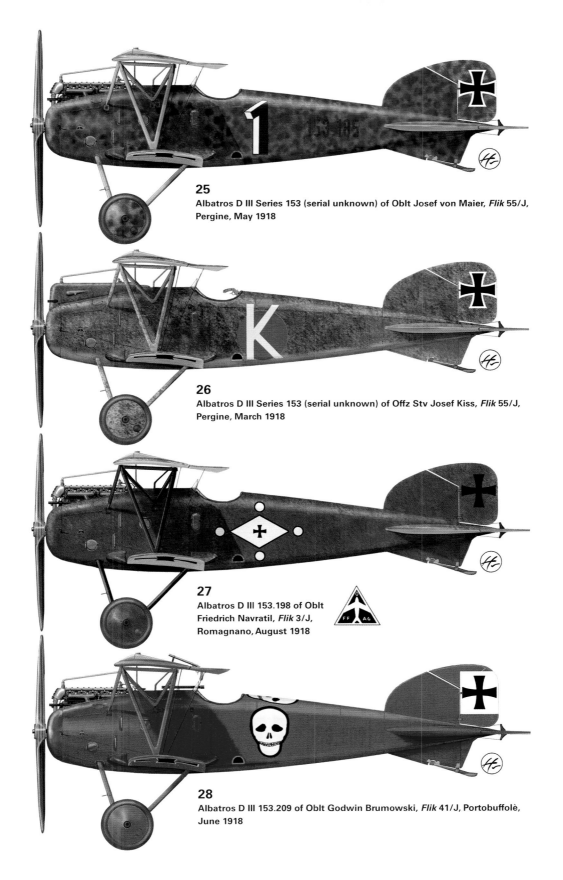

**25**
Albatros D III Series 153 (serial unknown) of Oblt Josef von Maier, *Flik* 55/J,
Pergine, May 1918

**26**
Albatros D III Series 153 (serial unknown) of Offz Stv Josef Kiss, *Flik* 55/J,
Pergine, March 1918

**27**
Albatros D III 153.198 of Oblt
Friedrich Navratil, *Flik* 3/J,
Romagnano, August 1918

**28**
Albatros D III 153.209 of Oblt Godwin Brumowski, *Flik* 41/J, Portobuffolè,
June 1918

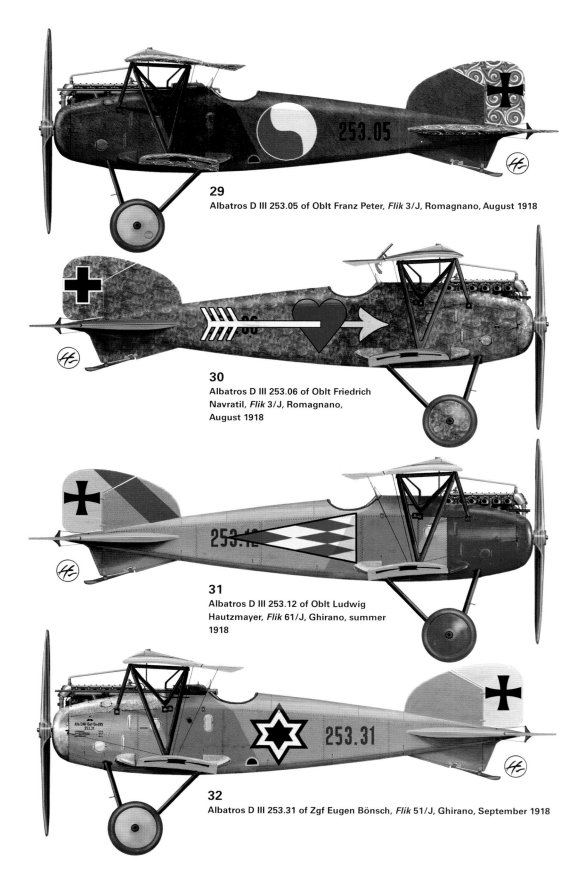

**29**
Albatros D III 253.05 of Oblt Franz Peter, *Flik* 3/J, Romagnano, August 1918

**30**
Albatros D III 253.06 of Oblt Friedrich
Navratil, *Flik* 3/J, Romagnano,
August 1918

**31**
Albatros D III 253.12 of Oblt Ludwig
Hautzmayer, *Flik* 61/J, Ghirano, summer
1918

**32**
Albatros D III 253.31 of Zgf Eugen Bönsch, *Flik* 51/J, Ghirano, September 1918

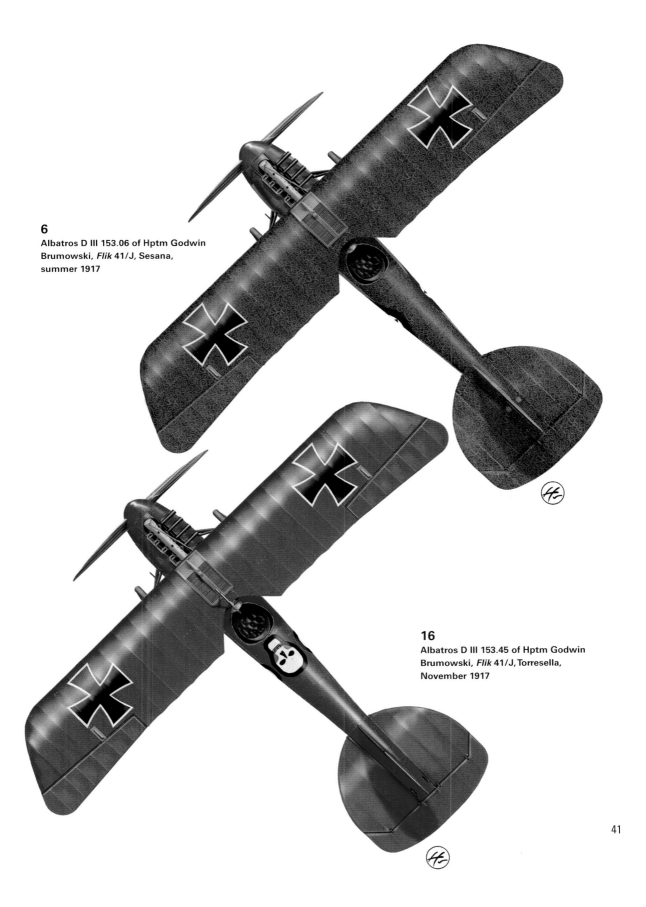

**6**
Albatros D III 153.06 of Hptm Godwin
Brumowski, *Flik* 41/J, Sesana,
summer 1917

**16**
Albatros D III 153.45 of Hptm Godwin
Brumowski, *Flik* 41/J, Torresella,
November 1917

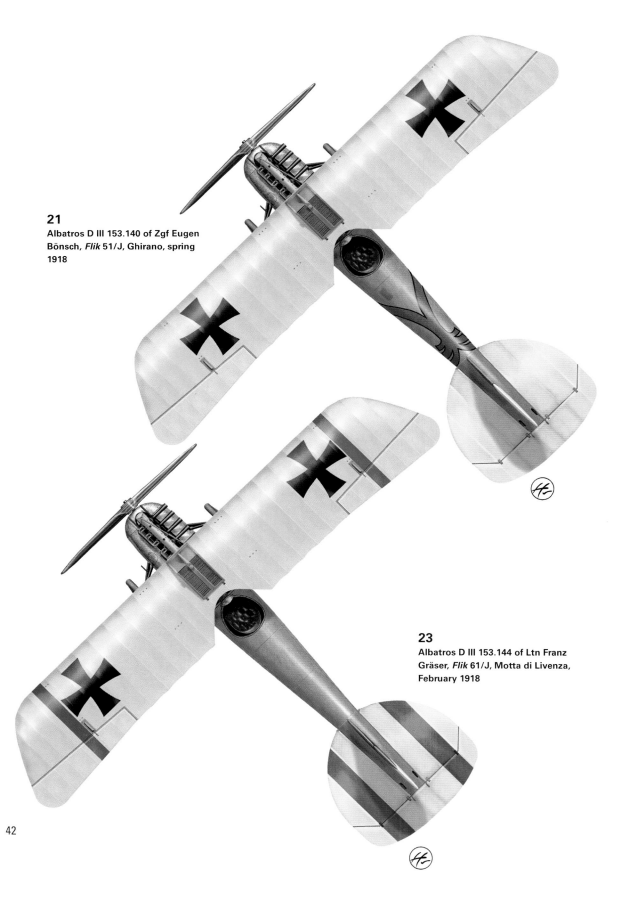

**21**
Albatros D III 153.140 of Zgf Eugen
Bönsch, *Flik* 51/J, Ghirano, spring
1918

**23**
Albatros D III 153.144 of Ltn Franz
Gräser, *Flik* 61/J, Motta di Livenza,
February 1918

According to some sources this photograph portrays StFw Josef Kiss flying over a glacier in the summer of 1917 in D III 53.33. This fighter, piloted by Kowalczik, was damaged and forced to land on 24 August by three SPADs of *71ª Squadriglia*. After repair it was returned in service, but was shot down once and for all on 29 November near Osteria Fontanelle by Soldato Clemente Panero of *82ª Squadriglia* killing *Rittermeister* Nikolaus Hideghety von Hideghet, commanding officer of *Flik* 24 *(Jiri Rajlich)*

'I took off from Casoni airfield (Bassano) at 0800 hrs, because at 0830 hrs I had to be at altitude over the entrance of the Valsugana. There, I would meet a fighter aeroplane that would escort me. However, it was not there. After a half-hour of useless waiting we started all the same. We crossed the barrage of fire from Monte Panarotta, from Busa Verle Fort, Cima 12, Spitz Verle Fort and Cima Mandrioli, taking some pictures and dropping leaflets near Levico and Pergine. After that, as we had decided before takeoff, we headed for the Astico Valley so as to return from that side. In this way we would avoid the self-propelled batteries of Ghertele, Verena and Monte Rovere that had hastened there for the Ortigara action.

'Then we saw about 1000 m under us an approaching enemy fighter, and some minutes later a first burst of machine gun fire came from behind. We immediately turned to have the adversary in front. So started the fight that would finish an hour later.

'The Austrian aeroplane was a "Tse-tse" fighter [in Italy it was said of a very insistent and tormenting person "He is even worse than a tse-tse fly!" Ed.], capable of a speed of 175 km/h [110 mph]. At the beginning we were able to cope with it, as much to force it more than once to withdraw to try again. But after a little while another aircraft came to help it – a "Brandenburg" armed with two machine guns that immediately opened fire against us. In that way they encircled us. We tried to reach the lines fighting, but soon some control cables were hit by bullets which prevented me from manoeuvring sharply, and I said to the observer with a wave of the hand to fire rearwards while we tried to escape. One of the aeroplanes attacked us from the front, barring us from flying in that direction. He saw that we were not changing route, so he moved on the flank and, from 30 m [100 ft], he launched bursts of fire against us.

'A bullet hit the observer on the upper lip and, while he was standing up continuing to fire with one hand and waving at me with the other, another bullet hit him in the head, piercing it from the right temple to the left cheek. Others hit the wings in several places. Tenente Semplicini of the 8th Infantry [Regiment] fell immediately and did not move any more.

'Then I tried to escape, but as I arrived over Levico more bullets fired from behind hit the main tank. I tried to use the reserve tank, but I discovered that it had been hit before. I came spiralling down so as not to strain the tail bracing wires that had been further damaged. I landed in an orchard near Levico Station because I was not able to reach an airfield near the lake.

'The first enemy aeroplane had landed just before me, I believe hit by the last bullets fired by my observer. When I asked about this, Fw Kiss (the second Austrian "ace") told me that he had had engine trouble. I was not able to set fire to my aircraft. I had a destructive flare, but it did not work. Before I was able to get the matches from under my flying gear I was encircled by soldiers from an infantry brigade that was resting in the city.'

The day before, on 12 July, two *Flik* 21 pilots had achieved their first confirmed victories whilst

The Albatros of *Alarm Bereitschaft Pergine* had a different nose colour. The second aircraft from the left, D III 53.29, was credited with four victories with four different pilots – Kpl Stephan Deutsch of *Flik* 21 on 10 July 1917, Ltn Johann Freiherr von Morpurgo of *Flik* 21 on 18 August, Zgf Ludwig Telessy of *Flik* 21 on 26 September and Ltn Josef Friedrich of *Flik* 24/F on 3 November. By 1918 53.29 was in service with the *Feldfliegerschule* in Egna, with whom it was eventually written off in an accident *(Carlo Lucchini)*

flying an Albatros fighter. Zgf Ludwig Telessy, in Albatros D III 53.39, and Fw Josef Kropf took off from Pergine airfield with a Brandenburg C I of the same unit, carrying as its observer Oblt Max Cavallar Ritter von Grabensprung, who had to perform a reconnaissance mission over Monte Zingarella, which was behind the Italian lines. As the formation neared the front the Austro-Hungarians met three aeroplanes, which they identified as Italian Nieuports. The Albatros pilots subsequently claimed a victory against one of them, the aircraft having reportedly crashed to the ground in a forest south of Cesuna, although there is no trace of such a loss in Italian records.

On 25 July the *LFT* issued instructions to identify the units according to their tasks by adding a letter to their number, 'J' (*Jagd* – fighter) being used for the fighter *Flik*s. The new organisation provided for 18 aircraft for the pure fighter units, divided in three *Kette* (flights) of six, with six pilot officers and 12 non-commissioned pilot officers. Chronic shortages of personnel and aeroplanes often meant that these specified strengths were rarely met. The non-fighter units continued to have one or two aircraft to escort their two-seaters.

Meanwhile, on the Isonzo Front, another outstanding pilot had been issued with his first Albatros fighter. On 18 July 1917 Hptm Godwin Brumowski, commander of *Flik* 42/J and already a leading Austro-Hungarian ace with 16 confirmed victories, took off for his first operational flight in the type. Born in Wadowice, now in Poland, on 26 July 1889, Brumowski chose a military career. After passing through the *Technische Militärakademie* he was assigned as leutnant to *Feldkanonenregiment 29*.

When war broke out he fought on the Russian Front with *Reitende Artillerie Division Nr. 6* until July 1915, when he joined *Flik* 1 as an observer, wearing on his chest the Bronze and Silver Military Merit Medals. Flying with this unit, Oblt Brumowski obtained his first confirmed victories in the spring of 1916 while manning the Schwarzlose machine gun in the observer's position of an Albatros B I. In July of that same year, after training, he received his field pilot's badge. Four months later he was transferred to the Italian Front, gaining his first victory as a pilot on 3 December. The command's esteem grew with his successes, and Brumowski, now an ace, was chosen to lead the first fighter unit of the *LFT*. But first he was instructed to go to the Western Front to study German fighter combat techniques, meeting the already famous Manfred von Richthofen.

Ltn Josef Friedrich of *Flik* 24 formates with the aeroplane that he escorted on 18 August 1918, when he claimed his eighth confirmed victory near Grigno. 53.38 was later assigned to *Flik* 48, and Zgf Michael Messner was flying it when he claimed a Nieuport near Thiene on 23 November *(Jiri Rajlich)*

Three aces and a fighter (plus a dog). The crew of the *45ᵃ Squadriglia* Savoia-Pomilio shot down on 23 August 1917 by three *Flik* 41/J KD fighters flown by Hptm Godwin Brumowski, Oblt Frank Linke-Crawford and Kpl Heinrich Mayrbäurl pose with the Austro-Hungarian pilots and their mascot in front of Albatros D III 153.06 on Sesana airfield. They are, from left to right, Oblt Benno Fiala von Fernbrugg, Ltn Ivekovic (*Flik* 42/J Technical Officer), Mayrbäurl, observer Tenente Giulio Cesare Mazzarino, Brumowski and Linke-Crawford. Pilot Sergente Ermanno Maspina sits in the cockpit of the D III *(Greg VanWyngarden)*

As commanding officer of *Flik* 41/J in Sesana, on the Isonzo Front, Brumowski, promoted to hauptmann in May, was able to claim more victories with his faithful KD 28.69 while countering Italian aviation activity in support of their spring offensive.

The Italian Supreme Command was planning yet another attack along the Isonzo Front with forces even more powerful than it had used in May, and the first Hanriot HD 1 fighters had recently arrived at the front. To make things worse for the Austro-Hungarians, their precarious situation had become known to their adversaries owing to a document found on the body of a fallen airman. It said;

'The enemy's air force is three times ours. Single-seat fighter aircraft are particularly needed. Given the violent enemy action, each reconnaissance aircraft must be escorted by two fighters. The number of existing fighter aeroplanes speaks for itself, and demonstrates the inability to perform aerial reconnaissance in the number needed, and to react strongly to enemy raids.'

This did not mean that the war had become an easy task for the Italian airmen when they launched their attack on 17 August for what would be known as the 11th Isonzo Battle. The following day, Ltn Josef Friedrich obtained his eighth victory – the first in an Albatros fighter – when he claimed an Italian single-seater over Grigno. His opponent was probably a Nieuport of *79ᵃ Squadriglia*, because two pilots from this unit, Tenente Umberto Mazzini and Sergente Antonio Reali (a future 11-victory ace) had combats in that area, but both returned to their airfield.

Friedrich, a 21-year-old university student at the outbreak of the war,

Fw Josef Nowak sits in the cockpit of Albatros D III 53.60 of *Flik* 41/J, wearing a nightcap with a bow on his flying helmet. He shared with Brumowski the victories claimed on 17 July and 19 August 1917. The aircraft has a simple mount for the flare pistol fitted in the centre of the top wing to fire upwards *(Jiri Rajlich)*

The Albatros in this *Flik* 42/J line-up on Prosecco airfield in September 1917 display different personal markings. They are, from left, an unknown D III with a dark diamond, D III 153.09 with a white-fringed black circle, 153.58 with a red circle in a white triangle outlined in red and 153.42 with a black-fringed red heart. StFw Hefty flew war missions in 153.09 and 153.58 in the latter part of the year. The petrol drums carefully aligned on the grass have triangular roofs, probably to prevent the sun overheating the fuel *(Carlo Lucchini)*

had served in a *Kaiserschützen* regiment before becoming an observer in *Flik* 16, then based in Villach. Flying in the rear seat of Brandenburg C I 64.14, piloted by Hptm Raoul Stojsavljevic, he shared his first victory with another two-seater. Their victim was Farman 957 of *29ª Squadriglia*, whose crew was captured. Friedrich then took flying lessons, and his last two victories in *Flik* 16, on 17 April and 3 May 1917, were achieved as a pilot.

After that first flight in D III 53.27 in July, Brumowski had resumed flying KDs, but on 19 August he scored his first victory in an Albatros D III. During his first mission that day he had a fight with an Italian Army FBA flying boat of *2ª Squadriglia Idro* that had been sent to attack the Austro-Hungarian position on Mount Hermada. Although the FBA was forced to land on the sea, with its observer, Tenente Francesco Porro, hit in a leg, this claim was unconfirmed.

Brumowski took off for a second flight later that same day, this time in D III 153.06, in company with the KDs of Fw Josef Nowak and Kpl Heinrich Mayrbäurl. The *Kette* was patrolling the sky between Monfalcone and Gorizia when they met an Italian aircraft identified as a 'Caudron' and shot it down in flames within their own lines, near Ivangrad. According to Italian sources the aircraft brought down by the ace and his wingmen was an SP of *39ª Squadriglia*, whose crew, pilot Tenente Teodoro Lacava and observer Tenente Cesare Poccianti, died. This was not only Brumowski's first victory while flying an Albatros, but also the first victory credited to the new series 153 fighters.

A double was claimed by Brumowski on 20 August in two different flights, and again he alternated between an Albatros and a KD. During a patrol along the route Sesana-Monfalcone-Hermada-Gorizia-Sesana, flying his D III 153.106, the ace first clashed with a Caproni flight escorted by fighters. He then engaged an aircraft identified as a Caudron, which he claimed as shot down in the area between San Giovanni and Monfalcone, near the Adriatic coast, in cooperation with Fw Hermann Richter and Kpl Heinrich Mayrlbäurl. Having returned to his airfield, he took off again, this time in KD 28.69, with Zgf Ferdinand Jaschek, and the pair claimed a second Caudron near Vertojba.

Although these claims received official confirmation, the diaries of the Italian squadrons reveal that although the first aircraft – actually a Savoia-

Oblt Ludwig Hautzmayer warms the engine of Albatros D III 253.12. The aircraft bears the identification markings of *Flik* 61/J – a slanting red stripe on the tail and red wheel discs. Part of the nose was painted the same colour, while the fuselage pennant could be blue and white *(Ivo Michael Forti)*

Pomilio reconnaissance biplane of *38ª Squadriglia* – was hit, it was able to return to base. The Savoia-Pomilio was over Gorizia when it was attacked and hit by an enemy fighter, prompting its pilot, Sergente Emilio Lubiani, to put the machine into a steep dive toward the Sistiana Gulf to fool his opponent. He was then able to land back at his home airfield in spite of the aircraft being hit by 37 bullets. Capitano Renato Mazzucco, commanding officer of *38ª Squadriglia*, endorsed the recommendation that Lubiani be awarded the *Medaglia d'Argento al Valor Militare* – the second highest Italian award for military gallantry. The other machine, a Savoia-Pomilio of *35ª Squadriglia,* was hit by 14 bullets and forced to land near Casa Blanchis, with its crew unhurt.

19 August had also marked the first combat loss of an Albatros, with the death of Oblt Otto Jäger, an ace who claimed his seventh victory during his last fight. Jäger took off from Sesana in company with Fw Vinzenz Magerl to engage the Italian bombers that were targeting Mount Hermada. Intercepting a diving aeroplane that they identified as a Caudron near San Giovanni, Jäger went down to investigate. Moments later Magerl was bounced by an Italian SPAD VII piloted by Tenente Alberto Marazzani, who riddled his D III. Jäger immediately climbed in an attempt to help his comrade, but was hit by bullets fired from the SPAD VII of another Italian pilot of *77ª Squadriglia*, Tenente Giovanni De Briganti, and D III 153.14 lost a wing, crashing near Ivanigrad.

Jäger and Magerl, who was able to limp back to his airfield, were credited with a victory apiece, but from Italian sources we know that the two-seater (actually a Savoia-Pomilio SP.2 pusher, rather than a Caudron) managed to return to base. This was Magerl's fourth victory, and his first in an Albatros, and he received the *Silbernetapferkeitmedaille 2. Klasse*.

Born in 1891, Magerl had started his aviation career as a mechanic, and after pilot training was posted to *Flik* 6 in Albania, where he had had a bad experience on 8 November 1915. Flying with Ltn Hans Schweinburg as his observer, Magerl was forced to land in Montenegro and was captured, but he escaped on 26 January of the following year.

In the last days of the 11th Battle of Isonzo the newly created *Flik* 51/J began combat operations from Ajdussina. Originally assigned to *Heeresgruppe Conrad* in South Tyrol, the unit had been diverted to Ajdussina and duly became the most successful Albatros *Flik* in Royal and Imperial Austro-Hungarian aviation. Its

Two Albatros of *Flik* 61/J are serviced outside their fabric hangar on Portobuffolè airfield in the summer of 1918 *(Ivo Michael Forti)*

commanding officer, *Rittmeister* Wedige von Froreich of *Ulanenregiment 11*, had previously served as an observer and pilot in several *Flik*, and from May to June had flown DFWs and Albatros C Xs with the German *Fliegerabteilung* 18 on the Western Front. Froreich, who already had three victories to his name, claimed the first for his new unit on 26 August 1917 during a flight from Gorizia to Tolmein (now Tolmin, in Slovenia). The 'Nieuport monoplace' was officially credited to D III 53.54 and its pilot, but there are no known Italian losses.

On 21 September 1917 LschIt Gottfried Banfield, the commanding officer of the Triest Seaplane Station and ace of the Austro-Hungarian naval air service, visited his terrestrial colleagues in Sesana and took the opportunity to test D III 53.27. The spinner fitted to the Albatros fighter could sometimes suffer an in-flight failure that would in turn cause damage to the aircraft, so it was often removed as a precaution *(Greg VanWyngarden)*

The Italians continued their tireless raids behind the Austro-Hungarian lines, and during the afternoon of 28 August, 11 Caproni bombers of several units, in company with other aircraft types of the *III Armata*, left their airfields to drop about two-and-a-half tons of bombs on artillery sites and infantry near Vojscica. On the return leg Caproni Ca.4039, piloted by Tenente Gino Lisa and Caporale Arturo Vischioni, was attacked near Cerovljie by fighters that were faster than the escorting SPADs. Sergente Agostino Galli and Caporale Emilio Saletta manned the bomber's Fiat 6.5 mm machine guns, but the bullets fired by D IIIs 53.62, flown by Oblt Ludwig Hautzmayer of *Flik* 19, and 53.55, piloted by Oblt Josef Hoffmamm Ritter von Ostenhof, pierced the Caproni's petrol tanks and hit Galli, while Lisa had his clothes holed but remained unscathed. The pursuit ended over Duino when the Caproni crash-landed on Aiello airfield, from where Galli, wounded in the chest and head, was carried unconscious to a field hospital.

Caproni Ca.4039 was the fourth victory officially credited to Hautzmayer, a 23-year-old Styrian who, in the first part of the war, had fought on the Russian Front, initially as an infantryman and then as an observer with *Flik* 15.

The bomber crew reported that the aircraft were of a 'new type', and this led to the Albatros being officially recognised by the Italian aviation command the following day. Its records noted that 'the presence on our front of fighter aeroplanes of a new model with an approximate speed of 190 km/h [120 mph] and V-shaped interplane struts like Nieuports must be pointed out'. One person who had clearly seen the distinctive features of the D III during an escort mission for a group of Capronis was Maggiore Pier Ruggero Piccio, who was to end the war with 29 victories and subsequently become the first Chief of Staff of the *Regia Aeronautica*.

*Flik* 51/J claimed another victory on 1 September 1917 during a barrage-spotting flight along the frontline from Gorizia to Tolmino when a patrol led by Froreich engaged an aeroplane identified as a 'Nieuport' (it was possibly a Società Anonima Meccanica Lombarda [SAML] S.2 of *113ª Squadriglia*) over Monte San Gabriele. The aircraft returned to its airfield with pilot Sergente Mario Doria lightly wounded. In addition to the leader, this victory was also accredited to Oblt Josef Hoffmann von Ostenhof, Zgf Ludwig Neumann and Kpl Eugen Bönsch, a 20-year-old former aviation mechanic. Bönsch, born in Bohemia to German parents, had shown such skill in pilot training that he went straight from flying school to *Flik* 51/J. Highly praised by his comrades, he was a quiet and modest person who never spoke about the war, even in old age.

On 11 September the *Stoluft* of *11. Armee* confirmed the third victory of Zgf Telessy, who, flying Albatros D III 63.39, claimed the shooting down of a Farman near Primolano while escorting Brandenburg C I 129.29.

During the summer *Flik* 55/J began to operate Albatros scouts from Aidussina. Its pilots were mostly inexperienced, with the notable exception of Offz Stv Julius Arigi, who already had 12 confirmed victories to his name. Born in Tetschen (now Decin, in the Czech Republic) on 3 October 1895 into a family originally from Val Sugana, Arigi lost his parents when he was 14, and later earned his living as an apprentice electrician. The early flights of the Wright brothers thrilled him, but he could not afford the luxury of flying lessons. At Berlin-Johannisthal airfield in 1912 he met Melli Beese, Germany's first female pilot, and she advised the young enthusiast to enlist in the army. Two years later, on 26 November 1914, his dream came true and he was awarded pilot's licence No 172 by the Austro-Hungarian Aero Club.

Fw Arigi performed his first wartime sorties in the Balkans against the armies of Serbia and Montenegro, flying the Lohners of *Flik* 6 from Igalo airfield. During a ferry flight on 14 October 1915 he became lost in clouds and forced-landed owing to fuel starvation in the Poblicnica Valley, Montenegro, which was enemy territory. Captured, Arigi eventually escaped and returned to his unit some three months later. He stated that while he was captive in Podgorica he stole a Fiat limousine belonging to the King of Montenegro and drove at breakneck speed until he reached the Austro-Hungarian lines.

When Italy entered the war, Arigi (who already had seven victories to his name) fought the new adversary with his usual energy after he was moved to the Italian Front at the end of 1916. In the new theatre he initially served with *Fluggeschwader* 1, and then with *Flik* 41/J from 23 May to 16 August 1917, when he was transferred to *Flik* 55/J. By then Arigi had added 12 more victories to his tally.

During the morning of 15 September, Arigi, flying D III 153.15, fought with a SPAD that escaped, diving toward Mount San Gabriele. Although he received confirmation for the fighter's demise as his 13th official victory, the aeroplane of Italian ace Tenente Ferruccio Ranza returned safely to Santa Caterina airfield.

The loose Austro-Hungarian system used to confirm victories also sanctioned the two aeroplanes claimed near Kostanjevica on 23 September by Oblt Ernst Strohschneider and Zgf Ferdinand

*Flik* 51/J in Ajdussina, probably in September 1917. Albatros D III 153.36 (the first fighter on the right) was flown by Off Stv Julius Arigi, who gained four confirmed victories in it from September to November 1917. The next D III in line, 153.33, with a pennant on its fuselage, was flown at this time by *Rittmeister* Wedige von Froreich, while the capital 'N' painted on 153.38 (fourtht from right) identifies this Albatros as Zgf Ludwig Neumann's aircraft *(Aeronautica Militare Italiana)*

Udvardy of *Flik* 42/J, but in Italian documentation there is no trace of the loss of a SPAD and a Savoia-Pomilio – the alleged third and fourth victories of the pair.

Udvardy was born in Pressburg (now Bratislava, in Slovakia) in 1895, and after being drafted into the army he volunteered for the air service, being assigned to *Flik* 42/J following a brief period with *Flik* 10 on the Russian Front.

Like Otto Jäger, Strohschneider had been judged unfit for infantry service after suffering his third wound in fighting on the Russian Front, and served as an observer before undergoing pilot training. As the *Chefpilot* of *Flik* 42/J, he firmly believed in the division of social classes that plagued the Austro-Hungarian Empire, and his behaviour toward non-commissioned officers was often remembered decades after the war. Arigi told aviation historian Martin O'Connor in 1977, 'The separation of officer and non-officer was disruptive. Many officers managed to avoid this and treated the NCOs well. Of all the officers I flew with, Strohschneider was the worst to the non-officers'.

High-scoring ace Oblt Frank Linke-Crawford had an entirely different personality, and enjoyed very good relationships with non-commissioned officers. Born in Crakow of a career officer and a British mother on 18 August 1893, he followed in his father's footsteps, volunteering in the *Wiener-Neustader Militärakademie* and then leaving it in 1913 for the *Dragonerregiment Friedrich Franz IV. Großherzog von Mecklenburg-Schwerin Nr. 6*, where he attained the rank of leutnant. The harsh conditions of the Russian Front took their toll on the young officer's health, and Linke asked to be transferred to aviation.

After serving in *Flik* 22 as an observer he obtained his pilot's licence and was sent in January 1917 to *Flik* 12 as *Chefpilot*. Flying as a reconnaissance pilot, Linke improved his skill, luckily escaping unhurt from crash landings after being attacked by Italian aces Baracca and Piccio on two occasions (1 May and 2 August 1917). In the first instance his aeroplane, Brandenburg C I 229.08 was recovered, but in the second his Aviatik C I 37.08 was eventually destroyed by Italian artillery.

In a photograph probably taken during *Kaiser* Karl I's visit to Pergine airfield on 14 September 1917, a D III overflies the automobile convoy of the august guest. It was common practice on both sides of the front to fly patrol missions to avoid unwelcome disturbances of the ceremony on such occasions *(Antonio Iozzi)*

Two days later Linke joined *Flik* 41/J and began his career as a fighter pilot, claiming four victories from 21 to 26 August in KD 28.40. For his fifth success, on the afternoon of 23 September, Linke-Crawford flew Albatros D III 153.04. His quarry, almost certainly a Macchi M.5 flying boat fighter, had taken off from Grado to escort a Macchi L.3 flying boat tasked with performing a photographic reconnaissance of Trieste. Once over the target area the pair were engaged by anti-aircraft fire, but this did not prevent the L.3 crew from taking their photographs and then heading for home.

The arrival at the front of the new Albatros fighters did not mean the end of war service for the Brandenburg D I. In this photograph of Pergine airfield, six Albatros, one KD and at least two Aviatik C Is await inspection by *Kaiser* Karl I on 14 September 1917. Ten days later, on the 24th, D III 53.51, piloted by Kpl Julius Früwirth, was involved in a fight over Monte Verena with a Nieuport flown by Sergente Antonio Amantea (a future five-victory ace). The Albatros was severely damaged and Früwirth was forced to land near Terlano. Although he was unscathed, Früwirth suffered nervous shock. The building on the hill, Villa Rosa, then used as quarters for *Flik* personnel, now houses a hospital *(Jiri Rajlich)*

Just as the flying boats were departing Trieste, 2º Capo Timoniere Luigi Zoni, flying the escort flying boat, saw enemy aircraft taking off from Sesana and made the fatal error of turning back to face them. The bursts fired by Linke quickly set the Macchi ablaze, and it crashed in the sea off Santa Croce, killing its pilot.

On 26 September Strohschneider and Udvardy became aces, obtaining confirmation for a SPAD claimed near Ronchi, behind Italian lines – it was shared with Magerl and Kpl Karl Teichmann. There were no Italian losses recorded on this day, however, their adversary possibly being Tenente Enrico Ferreri, who was attacked by four enemy aircraft but was able to escape and return to his airfield with his aircraft holed by a single bullet.

The military career of 20-year-old Teichmann, a Silesian, had started modestly with him serving as a car mechanic in *Infanterieregiment* 1. He was then moved to *Flik* 15 at the beginning of 1916 as an '*Apparate-Chauffeur*' (aeroplane mechanic), before finally obtaining a seat in the cockpit in August 1917.

Another victory on 26 September that received official confirmation was the 'SPAD' claimed by Telessy near Turcio, in the Asiago sector. Escorting a *Flik* 21/D Brandenburg on a photo-reconnaissance mission, he spotted two enemy aeroplanes and engaged them in combat, believing he had sent one down to crash. However, in the meantime, the other fighter had been free to engage the *LFT* two-seater, which was shot down in flames. Actually, Albatros D III 53.29 and Brandenburg C I 129.29 had been attacked by two *79ª Squadriglia* Nieuports piloted by Tenente Umberto Mazzini and Sergente Attilio Imolesi, who returned to their airfield unhurt. In its monthly report *Flik* 21/D complained of the increasing danger posed by long-range flights over enemy territory during this period, using the grim fate of C I 129.29's crew as an example.

Up to this time only aeroplanes had fallen to the Albatros fighters, but on 29 September a D III shot down the type's first '*draken*' (kite balloon No 187 of *9ª Sezione Aerostatica*), which burst into flames near Plava after being hit by the incendiary bullets fired by Bönsch and Ltn Alexander Tahy. The latter, a Hungarian officer, was born in 1896 in Nyiregyhaza. Like many of his fellow pilots, Tahy gained his first experiences of aerial warfare whilst serving as an observer. The balloon's Italian observer, Tenente Paolo Calisse, took to his parachute to escape the flaming hydrogen and walked away unhurt.

Tahy scored again the following day to gain his seventh victory, shooting down, again with Bönsch, the SPAD VII of Sergente Giuseppe Tesio of *77ª Squadriglia* near Plava.

In this period, just before what would become known as the 12th Isonzo Battle, the *LFT's* fighter units increased their attacks against Italian observation balloons, and on 9 October Brumowski, Linke and StFw Kurt Gruber destroyed the *10ª Sezione Aerostatica* kite balloon moored near Isola Morosini. Skilfully taking advantage of fog in the area, the three Albatros pilots came inland from Panzano Gulf in spite of the barrage of fire from the 76 mm guns of the Navy Alberoni battery, which was immediately targeted by Austro-Hungarian artillery, wounding two sailors. While the ground personnel frantically operated the winch to lower the balloon and the anti-aircraft machine gun opened fire, Brumowski and his wingmen headed bravely for the balloon. Their bullets set ablaze the gas when the *'draken'* was still at 800 m (2600 ft), and the observers, Tenenti Pier Felice Crostarosa and Alfredo Silenzi, had to entrust their lives to their parachutes.

The *Flik* 41/J patrol now had to face a SPAD drawn there by the anti-aircraft fire. Italian pilot Sergente Cosimo Rizzotto, who had already scored four of his total of six victories, wrote in his combat report;

'At the beginning I could not see any enemy aircraft. I came down to about 1000 m [3300 ft] and then an enemy fighter aeroplane coloured bright brick red, with black crosses on the wings, passed under me, flying towards the sea. I threw myself into pursuit, firing bursts from my machine gun. I reached it and forced it to come down, always firing, until I was only a few metres above the water. At that moment I became aware that my engine was malfunctioning, and turned to come back, but it stopped immediately, forcing me to land on swampy ground near Matarussi. I fired about 150 machine gun bullets and the enemy answered repeatedly to my fire.'

Gruber, the son of a teacher in Linz, Austria, had shot down three Russian aeroplanes while serving with *Flik* 1, prior to his move to the Italian Front, where he had obtained a fourth confirmed victory near Cormons on 29 September 1917. With this *'draken'* he achieved ace status. Gruber was subsequently shot down and killed on 4 April 1918 near Cismon, flying Phönix D I 228.24, by a No 66 Sqn patrol led by Capt F S Symondson.

Linke had a minor incident on 9 October when he overturned his D III, 153.04, upon landing at Sesana. Given 153.11 as a replacement, he used this fighter on 23 October to down a Savoia-Pomilio of *38ª Squadriglia*, which crashed on the eastern side of Mount Hermada, killing the pilot, Tenente Innocente Burello, and observer Tenente Francesco D'Audino.

StFw Kurt Gruber in front of an Albatros. Before his death he was awarded the Gold Bravery Medal (four times) and the Silver Medal (twice). His father, Josef, subsequently served as Mayor of Linz for the Social-Democratic Party from 1930 to 1934 *(Greg VanWyngarden)*

On 9 October 1917 Oblt Linke-Crawford flipped over his D III 153.04 while landing at Sesana airfield. Here, he poses, hands in pockets, in front of the wreck. To his right, an armourer holds one of the machine gun belts removed from the fighter. On that day Linke-Crawford, who had already obtained a confirmed victory in this aeroplane on 23 September, had claimed an Italian *'draken'* with Gruber and Brumowski and a SPAD by himself. The serial painted on the fuselage of this fighter of Flik 41 seems to have been scraped away *(Greg VanWyngarden)*

By the time this photograph was taken on 9 October 1917, ground personnel had righted 153.04, thus revealing its uppersurfaces. These had been camouflaged in the field in a scheme now named the 'Brumowski pattern' by World War 1 aviation historians. Brush swirls of a lighter colour, probably yellow, were carefully applied onto the dark green background *(Greg VanWyngarden)*

An informal study of Linke-Crawford, wearing his favourite light trousers, by the insignia that earned him the nickname 'The Falcon of Feltre'. Four victories were claimed by the airman with this aeroplane in just a month, from 23 October to 23 November 1917 *(Carlo Lucchini)*

During that month adverse weather hampered or prevented flying for about two weeks in total, but even darker clouds were gathering, this time on the Italian side only.

At 0200 hrs on 24 October the first gas and explosive shells used by the Austro-Hungarians began to rain down on the Italian lines near Tolmino, hitting trenches, artillery positions and shelters, and killing men and beasts, devastating the battlefield and cutting communications. While the Italian retreat was becoming a rout, the *Fliks* were forced to remain on their airfields by the strong Bora wind, and they could not intervene until 25 October. On that date they hit troops that were marching westwards and clashed with disorganised formations of Italian aircraft, whose crews fought with the courage of desperation.

From 25 October to 7 November 1917, when the Italian Army established new lines of defence on the Piave River, *LFT* airmen flying single-seaters claimed 19 victories – 12 with the Albatros, three on Aviatik D Is, two with the old KDs still in service and two on unknown types.

During the morning of 25 October Strohschneider shared his seventh victory with Ltn Franz Gräser, claiming a seaplane near the mouth of the Piave River. Gräser, born in the Hungarian city of Nyírmada on 18 October 1892, was a student in the technical university of Budapest at the beginning of the war. After a tour of duty as a machine gun officer on the Russian Front, during which he was wounded, he volunteered for the flying service, and in October 1916, after training, was assigned to *Flik* 2 as an observer, obtaining his first victories with this unit.

Moved to *Flik* 32 in May 1917, he took flying lessons and joined *Flik* 42/J as a fighter pilot on 1 October. During the afternoon of 26 October Gräser claimed a double in the forms of a *'draken'* and an Italian Nieuport, and on the same day Strohschneider obtained his eighth victory, sharing a seaplane downed into the Grado Lagoon with Zgf Ferdinand Udvardy.

At about 1015 hrs the following day, in spite of bad weather, Strohschneider claimed another seaplane in the same location, this time with Gräser, who was flying D III 153.13.

On 3 November Friedrich claimed a kite balloon near Monte Pau, in the northern sector, flying D III 53.29 of *Flik* 21/D to gain his ninth victory.

Although all 19 claims made between 25 October and 7 November 1917 were officially homologated as victories, the only known Italian losses that could be ascribed to the Albatros pilots were the Italian flying boats shot down by Brumowski, Linke and Szepessy-Sokoll on 5 November. On that day

a formation of Macchi L.3s took off from Venice seaplane station to attack the boat bridges made by Austro-Hungarian engineers to span the Tagliamento River. Over the target L.3 M.4862, piloted by Tenente Arnaldo De Filippis, commanding officer of *251ª Squadriglia*, was bounced by three Albatros of *Flik* 41/J. The Macchi M.5 fighter flying boats of *260ª Squadriglia*, which was making its operational debut, tried to assist their comrades and noted a bright red Albatros, but the L.3 crashed into a swamp, killing De Filippis and his observer, Tenente di Vascello Francesco Cappa. The Austro-Hungarian pilots then encountered a second L.3 that was returning after a flight over Portogruaro, where the crew had dropped a message. Macchi M.4842, crewed by Marinaio Luigi Bruzzone and his observer Sottotenente di Vascello Luigi D'Orso, had its radiator pierced but was able to glide toward Baseleghe, where it alighted, protected by anti-aircraft fire from the Italian pontoons.

The Italians had lost thousands of men and a huge quantity of material during the 12th Isonzo Battle. However, they had also discovered a new will to fight, thus slowly pushing back their adversaries.

During the morning of 6 November five-victory ace Szepessy-Sokoll took off with his wingman, Fw Radames Iskra, and headed west. Near Portogruaro they met two SPAD VIIs from the crack Italian *91ª Squadriglia*, piloted by leading Italian ace Maggiore Francesco Baracca and Tenente Giuliano Parvis, a future ace then with three victories to his credit. Iskra, after a brief fight with Parvis, chose to desert, fled and landed near Treviso, giving his intact fighter to the Italians. His leader, who was alone and at low altitude, tried to foil his opponents by spiralling down, but at tree-top height he had to level out and was hit. Severely wounded in the back, Szepessy-Sokoll crash-landed in a final effort, but died as he was being lifted from the cockpit by his rescuers.

While the Austro-Hungarian *Flik* moved to airfields close to the new frontline, and British and French troops accompanied aviation units to reinforce the Italian Army, the

**Doomed Macchi L.3 M4842 of *251ª Squadriglia* on the apron of the seaplane station in Venice. This flying boat was shot down on 5 November 1917 by the D IIIs of Brumowski, Linke-Crawford and Oblt Rudolf Szepessy-Sokoll (*Marina Militare Italiana*)**

**The upper wing of D III 153.54 collapsed when the fighter hit the ground near Portogruaro on 6 November 1917. Rescuers could do nothing for its pilot, ace Szepessy-Sokoll, who died shortly after the crash-landing, as he had been hit in the back by a bullet fired during combat with Italian 'ace of aces' Francesco Baracca and his wingman Tenente Giuliano Parvis (six victories by war's end). Baracca wrote in a letter that the enemy aeroplane had a black band painted around its fuselage (*Antonio Iozzi*)**

The relaxed attitude of Hptm Josef von Maier and his subordinates in this photograph, taken at Pergine on 7 January 1918, suggests that he was able to create a sense of comradeship in *Flik* 55/J that went beyond rank and social status – a very rare thing in the Austro-Hungarian armed forces. Von Maier is in the centre, with Munczar and Lehmann on his right, while Fw Alfons Behounek, lying on top of the fuselage, plays with the nightcap worn by Lahner, sitting in the cockpit. Albatros number '8' is probably D III 153.100, which was shot down on 21 March 1918 by the Hanriot HD 1s flown by *76ª Squadriglia* aces Tenenti Silvio Scaroni (second in the Italian ace list, with 26 victories) and Giorgio Michetti (five victories). The Albatros' pilot, Munczar, was uninjured, and he later joined the Czechoslovak Legion that fought on the Allied side *(Bohumir Kudlicka)*

fight moved to the mountain sector – now the mainstay of the Allied defensive line.

*Flik* 55/J, commanded by Hptm Josef von Maier, a 28-year-old career officer born in Bratislava of Hungarian parents, had arrived in Pergine in October 1917. As an observer in a *Flik* 14 Lohner B V piloted by Zgf Johann Varga, Maier had had a narrow escape in the very first weeks of the war when they were forced to land inside Russian lines owing to engine failure. The airmen kept their cool, set fire to their biplane and crossed the front, in spite of the Cossack patrols. After pilot training and a further tour of duty on the Russian and Rumanian fronts, Maier learnt to fly fighters and was appointed commanding officer of *Flik* 55/J. Into the unit came the best pilots of the *Alarm - Bereitschaft* such as Kiss and Arigi.

On 15 November 1917 Maier, Kiss and Arigi together gained the first success of a series that earned the trio the nickname *Kaiser Staffeln* (Kaiser's Squadron). Near Caldonazzo they saw three Caproni tri-motor bombers in vee formation and attacked the leading one. In Ca.4169 of *10ª Squadriglia* were pilots Tenente Luigi Garrone and Sergente Rosario Zingales, with gunners Soldati Bruno Manfredi and Natale Coccé. The latter, manning the rear gun, was severely wounded by the first burst, and bullets pierced the petrol tanks, radiator and spars, and damaged the central and port engines. The Caproni pilots dropped their bombs on the first target they saw and limped back on a single engine, while the crew tried to stop the fuel leaks with their gloves. They managed to crash-land the bomber near Montecchio Maggiore, and Coccé was carried to hospital, but died on the operating table.

An Austro-Hungarian soldier poses near the wreck of an overturned Caproni bomber that probably tried to crash-land with dead engines. The violence of the impact has opened the bomb doors under the nacelle *(Bohumir Kudlicka)*

Meanwhile, the Albatros trio had attacked and shot down Caproni Ca.4191 of *2ª Squadriglia*, whose crew, pilots Tenente Gino Lisa, Sergente Maggiore Guido Colli, observer Tenente Peitro Bassi and gunner Soldato Carlo Tagliabue, all perished. The fight was witnessed by several Italian officers on the ground, who gave the following details pertaining to the bomber's demise;

'Aeroplane 4191 was seen heading south from Cengio, chased by three enemy fighters. It defended itself with dogged tenacity with tight turns and spirals, always firing with the machine guns. When it was over Meda at about 1000 m [3300 ft], our Caproni was seen to capsize and spin. The rear gunner was thrown from the aeroplane and fell on the northern side of Monte Summano, near the houses of the Crosara hamlet (on the street between Meda and Val d'Astico). After a few seconds our aeroplane straightened its flight path, leaving a great smoke plume, probably trying to go over the ridge that runs down toward Meda from Monte Summano, but it crashed against the ridge, killing the crew.'

A Savoia-Pomilio two-seater accredited to two other pilots of *Flik* 55/J, Fw Alois Lehman and Zgf Alexander Kasza, as their first victory on that same day near Bassano is not confirmed in Italian records. Kasza, a Hungarian, had arrived at the unit in August 1917 after serving as a flying instructor in Fischamend, near Vienna.

There is also no trace of the 'Sopwith' claimed by Strohschneider and Gräser near Meolo, on the Piave Front.

There was a lot of action for the Austro-Hungarian airmen and their Italian counterparts on 17 November. Curiously, almost all of it happened at the same time, but over different parts of the battlefront.

At 1100 hrs a Savoia-Pomilio SP.3 of *26ª Squadriglia* had finished its reconnaissance mission and was heading for home when it was attacked by Arigi and Maier. In the SP.3's front cockpit, observer Tenente Mario Marangoni turned rearwards to keep an eye on the fighters, urging his pilot Sergente Aldo Alessandrini to escape from the pursuing aeroplanes. Finally, the two-seater was able to shake off the adversaries, although not before it had been hit by 27 incendiary bullets. Such was the damage inflicted by these shells that, after landing, the aircraft was written off.

Capitano Luigi Castiglioni, temporary commanding officer of *115ª Squadriglia*, and his observer, Tenente Umberto Benvegnù Pasini, in SAML S.2 2935 had less luck, being shot down and killed about ten minutes later near Cima Ecker. The aeroplane had been tasked with a strategic reconnaissance mission, and was escorted by two more SAML S.2s, but Castiglioni lost his wingmen and was seen from the ground to be attacked and shot down in flames by a single fighter. Maier and Arigi also gained confirmation for a second SAML S.2, but this claim is not confirmed in Italian or Allied records.

A familiar image of Godwin Brumowski in full flying gear near the black-shrouded skull painted on his D III, 153.52. Visible to the right of the ace's head are the light 'tresses' added to Brumowski's favourite overall red scheme. This fighter was accepted by the *LFT* on 13 September 1917, reached *Flik* 41/J on 14 October and was formally written off in June 1918 *(Koloman Mayrhofer)*

At about the same time on the opposite side of the front, in Portegrandi, near Quarto d'Altino, Brumowski set ablaze *'draken'* SCA Nº 143, but its crew – Capitano Romeo Landini, commanding officer of *20ª Sezione Aerostatica*, and Tenente Guido Vendittelli – escaped by parachute.

Almost simultaneously, about ten kilometres (six miles) to the north, von Froreich claimed a 'Sopwith' near San Biagio. This was the aircraft flown by Sergente Maggiore Oreste Bontempi, who was forced to crash-land with a dead engine.

Finally, in the early afternoon, Kasza gained his second 'victory', sharing a Nieuport over Valstagna with Ltn Egbert Lupfer and Offz Stv Emanuel Stumpa. However, they had probably mistaken the manoeuvres of Italian ace Attilio Imolesi, who was forced to leave the fight and return to his airfield after his machine gun jammed.

On 18 November, in the sky over the Asiago Plateau, there was a crowded fray between a strong *Flik* 55/J patrol and Italian reconnaissance aeroplanes and their escorts. The Austro-Hungarian pilots claimed a fighter near Villaverla (Oblt Georg Kenzian von Kenzianhausen, Lahner, Lupfer and Offz Stv Emanuel Stumpa), two two-seaters near Monte Cengio (Arigi and Maier) and a fighter and a two-seater near Arsiero (Kiss). According to official sources, the Italians lost an SVA (Sergente Bartolomeo Arrigoni of *1ª Sezione SVA*, who escaped unhurt from the burning wreck of his fighter in Villaverla) and two Savoia-Pomilio SPs (the aircraft of *31ª Squadriglia* crashed, killing Carabiniere Celso Botteghi and Tenente Ettore Bernardo, while the two-seater of *132ª Squadriglia* was destroyed in a crash-landing, observer tenente Remo Palazzo suffering wounds), while two SAML S.2s belonging to *121ª Squadriglia* were able to return home damaged.

The crash of SP.3 4518 of *31ª Squadriglia,* which had taken off at 1020 hrs for a reconnaissance flight over Val Lagarina and Val d'Astico, was observed by the officers of *141ª Reggimento Fanteria,* who recalled that at about 1140 hrs 'the SP aircraft had just arrived over the frontline (without crossing it) when it was resolutely attacked by at least four enemy machines. During a turn after a brief fight the aircraft caught fire – the nacelle broke away from the burning aeroplane and the two airmen fell out'. The bodies of the unfortunate crew were recovered by the regiment's chaplain and buried in the cemetery of Castelgomberto.

That day's successes received an involuntary tribute in the Historical Diary of the Italian aviation command, which noted, 'The unusual air activity shown by the adversary, and the painful effects produced by that, demonstrate the huge increase of the adversary's fighters on the front of the I Army'.

On 21 November Hptm Raoul Stoisavljevic gained his first victory with an Albatros fighter. He was the commanding officer of *Flik* 16/D, a divisional unit (as indicated by the suffix D) charged with supporting ground forces and artillery reconnaissance that also had some fighters within its inventory. That day he obtained his 12th victory, shooting down SAML S.2 2999 of *114ª Squadriglia*, crewed by pilot Tenente Mario Vannuccini and observer Tenente Antonio Mangano, near Quero. Austro-Hungarian artillery officer Hptm Bruno Schmidt witnessed the combat, and later wrote;

'On 21 November 1917, at 1500 hrs, an enemy medium aircraft was seen in the area of Quero, apparently directing the fire of a heavy battery against our batteries. At about 1515 hrs, I and all the people around saw the enemy aeroplane attacked by one of our pilots. The enemy was set ablaze by the fire from the machine gun of our pilot and dived steeply. The fire enveloped the whole aircraft. Both occupants fell out, burning, and the aeroplane crashed to the ground about 400 steps southwest of the church of Quero. One of the occupants was buried by German troops near the church.'

In this photograph, taken during the winter of 1917, Ltn Franz Gräser (far left) smiles with some visitors on Motta di Livenza airfield in front of his Albatros D III, 153.44. Peeping out behind the man with the walking stick is the eagle owl chosen by the ace as his personal insignia, painted in dark brown on a white background *(Carlo Lucchini)*

Early in the new year Stojsavljevic was awarded a cash prize of 1000 *Kronen* by *10. Armeekommando* for his success, and this was used to improve the food being served by the squadron mess. By then Stojsavljevic had been hospitalised with wounds inflicted in combat with aircraft from *66ª Squadriglia* near Seren on 12 January 1918.

'Iron Stoj', as he was nicknamed by his squadronmates, was a career officer born in Innsbruck on 29 July 1887. The son of Mladen, an artillery officer of Serbian nationality, he was among the first Austro-Hungarian military pilots, having received his licence in 1913. Stojsavljevic spent the first part of the war in Galicia with *Flik* 1, then moved to *Flik* 13 and, on 16 February 1915, became a prisoner of the Russians after his aircraft ran out of fuel. Stojsavljevic did not lose heart and escaped six days later, hiding in Lemberg (now Lvov, in Ukraine) until the arrival of Austro-Hungarian and German troops four months later. Sent to the Italian Front in 1915, he became commanding officer of *Flik* 16 in December 1916. In February of the following year Stojsavljevic learnt to fly a fighter with *Flik* 34, spending time on the Western Front with *Jasta* 6 in order to sharpen his skills with his German colleagues.

Brumowski and Gräser claimed a double on 23 November near the mouth of the Piave River, but there is no corresponding loss recorded in Allied documentation. This was also the case for the fighter that Kasza believed he had shot down near Rubbia (he probably encountered Parvis and Tenente Guido Keller of *91ª Squadriglia*, who returned to their airfield) and the single-seater credited to Oblt Karl Patzelt and Kpl Karl Teichmann after yet another fight over the Piave River. In the latter clash, high-scoring ace Maggiore Piccio was able to land his badly damaged SPAD on Istrana airfield.

This was Teichmann's third success in an Albatros. He then moved to *Flik* 60/J, where he gained two more victories flying the Phönix D I. He survived the war but died in 1927 in Graz, aged just 30.

On the same date, 23 November, the circumstances surrounding the deaths of Tenenti Egidio Grego and Pietro Baggio in Macchi L.3 M.4386 of *253ª Squadriglia* match perfectly the victory claimed by Gräser and Zgf Paul Jelinek near Agenzia. The flying boat had taken off from Venice to direct the fire of Royal Navy monitors in the area, but it was set on fire by the Albatros fighters' Schwarzlose bullets and Baggio jumped from the L.3 in order to escape the flames. The pilot's body was later recovered by a patrol of *Arditi* (Italian assault troops). 'Egidio Greco' was actually Attilio Munari, an Austro-Hungarian subject with Italian sympathies who had changed his name to escape the gallows if captured. Interestingly, the Italians ascribed the victory to Brumowski.

On 25 November another naval pilot based at Venice, Guardiamarina Paolo Morterra of *260ª Squadriglia*, wrote;

'The other day I had a terrible fight with Brumowski, the Austro-Hungarian ace who, unfortunately, has 30 victories. The enemy fighters (there were three) took us by surprise and attacked us so quickly (the speed of their aeroplanes is 220 km/h [140 mph]) that one of our aircraft was shot down in flames.'

The respect for their adversaries, which perhaps drifted into involuntary admiration, was also felt by Brumowski, who, according to a note in the *LFT Nachrichtenblatt* (the official bulletin of Austro-Hungarian aviation) published on 25 October 1917, had said to a German journalist who was interviewing him, 'The Italian pilots are brave and skilful, though on several occasions only two Austrian pilots were attacked by a whole squadron of enemy aeroplanes'.

On 27 November Hptm Karl Nikitsch was credited with his first victory while flying Albatros D III 153.71. That morning Nikitsch, the 32-year-old commanding officer of *Gruppenflieger der Korpsgruppe Krauss*, attached to the *14. Armee*, left the latter's headquarters in Vittorio Veneto and arrived by car at Aviano, a former Italian airfield, to take off in a *Flik* 39 aircraft. In the sky over Monte Grappa, he claimed an Italian two-seater that was confirmed by several eyewitnesses on the ground. It is possible that these observers actually verified the crash-landing of a Savoia-Pomilio from *27ª Squadriglia*, which was forced down near Cornuda after receiving an anti-aircraft shell splinter in its petrol tank. The observer in this reconnaissance aeroplane, piloted by Sergente Carlo Fenocchio, was Tenente Silvio Paolo Palli, brother of Natale, who would subsequently fly Italian poet Gabriele d'Annunzio on his famous leaflet-dropping mission over Vienna in August 1918.

Whatever the identity of his victim, this success proved to be Nikitsch's sixth, and last, victory, for on 18 January 1918, while leading *Flik* 63/J, he was severely wounded in a crash. After hospitalisation, Nikitsch went to *Flieger-Lehr-Bataillon* in Wiener Neustadt as commanding officer, where he remained until war's end.

At 1230 hrs on 27 November two SAML S.2s of *115ª Squadriglia* took off from Nove di Bassano. The first was flown by Sottotenente Severo Milani, with Sottotenente Tullio Lovy as his observer. Crewing the second machine were Tenente Serafino Battaini and Sottotenente Stefano Achenza. The reconnaissance aircraft climbed over the airfield until 1330 hrs in order to reach 4000 m (13,000 ft). After being joined by two SPAD fighters of *71ª Squadriglia*, the SAML S.2s headed to Asiago. Their intended target was Albergo del Ghertele.

Shortly after the first shrapnel burst around them, the SAML S.2s lost their escort. Battaini subsequently reported;

'After about 15 minutes of observation of the area, and having just taken the last photograph of the reconnaissance, our aeroplane was suddenly attacked by a very fast single-seater enemy aircraft. We engaged in a lively fight that began at an altitude of 4000 m over Ghertele and finished 20 minutes later at a height of about 500 m (1600 ft) over Asiago. The enemy fighter, still under fire from our machine gun and now at low altitude near our lines, ceased the pursuit, perhaps also thinking he had hit us. [Our] aircraft returned to the field at 1450 hrs.'

A large black-and-white '2' and a white-and-blue pennant identified Albatros D III 153.27, flown by Oblt Georg von Kenzian of *Flik* 55/J in the last months of 1917. During this period the unit used large numerals or letters on the fuselage as insignia, often with other markings. It appears that the pilot of 153.27 had put its wheels in the shallow ditch to the left of the photograph and turned the fighter over onto its back (*Carlo Lucchini*)

The crew was unable to provide information about the fate of the other SAML S.2 because they had had 'to change height and area'. In fact SAML S.2 2952 had been attacked by Josef Kiss in D III 153.87 and Georg Kenzian in D III 153.27, who shot down the two-seater near Cima Ecker. The victory was confirmed by the Aviation Headquarters of the *11. Armee*, which also ascribed to Kiss the shooting down of a second aircraft, misinterpreting Battaini's desperate evasive manoeuvres for an aircraft spiralling down out of control.

SAML S.2 2952 was Kenzian's fifth official victory, giving him ace status. Born in the Bohemian city of Jicin (now in the Czech Republic) on 11 May 1894, the son of a career officer, he too had been a career officer pre-war. In the first part of the conflict he had fought on the Russian Front as a leutnant in an Engineer Battalion, being wounded on 18 December 1914. After recovering, Kenzian returned to combat and was promoted to oberleutnant in September of the following year. He volunteered for the aviation service and underwent the observer's course at the Wiener Neustadt school, before joining Pergine-based *Flik* 24 in the spring of 1916.

In the rear seat of a Brandenburg piloted by Fw Rudolf Forst, Kenzian claimed his first victory on 16 June 1916 near Asiago. During the morning of 27 July the aeroplane in which Kenzian was flying with Zgf Alois Jezek (Brandenburg C I 61.23) was badly damaged by bullets fired by an Italian biplane, and it was forced to land within Austro-Hungarian lines. It is almost certain that they had fallen victim to Tenente Carlo Savio and Sottotenente Ferruccio Ranza, a future ace with 17 confirmed victories, who reported fighting with a two-seater that was able to cross the frontline, and whose observer had been hit, losing his camera and notes, which were later found by the Italians. This victory was not claimed by the Italian airmen, and was therefore not included in the official listings. Kenzian, who had been badly wounded during this action, spent three months recovering.

Upon returning to the front, he was assigned in February 1917 to the Wiener Neustadt school as an instructor. There, he also received pilot training, and in August, a month after the awarding of his pilot's certificate, Kenzian joined *Flik* 55 as *Chefpilot*.

27 November was indeed an unlucky day for the Italians, who lost another SAML S.2. The aircraft, serial 3076, belonging to *121ª Squadriglia*, was shot down near Campomolon, on the Asiago Plateau, by two *Flik* 55 series 153 Albatros fighters flown by Lupfer and Lahner. Tenente Rodolfo Fumagalli and Tenente Piero Ghinozzi perished in the burning wreck of their aeroplane. Among known losses for the 27th there are no traces of the 'SP' claimed by Brumowski and Kaszala near Favaro or the two-seater claimed by Gräser over Montello.

Conversely, there is no doubt about the fate of SAML S.2 2495, claimed on 29 November near the mouth of the Piave by Strohschneider, Gräser and Patzelt. The crew of the Italian biplane, Sergente Francesco Montesi and Tenente Vincenzo Lioy, were captured unhurt, and the observer wrote a report when he returned from captivity in the concentration camp at Sigmundsherberg.

On that day three SAML S.2s of *115ª Squadriglia* had received orders to make a photographic reconnaissance of the bridges over the Tagliamento and Livenza rivers. As usual, crews of the two-seaters agreed the details of the mission with the four pilots of the escort fighters. Lioy, the patrol leader, who carried a tricolour ribbon on a wing strut, headed east, but when he arrived over Codroipo he discovered he was alone. The officer decided to continue, and although the sun was rapidly setting he gave Montesi a nod to fly toward the target. After they had taken their last photograph over the Livenza River, the pilot throttled the engine back to start the glide towards the Italian lines. It was at this point that three Albatros fighters were seen, with their national insignia clearly visible on their tails.

Quickly, the fighters encircled the SAML S.2 and Lioy 'started to use the machine gun [a Fiat Revelli] to hold the adversaries at bay and allow the pilot to reach the lines. However, after about 20 shots the Fiat jammed. Then the pilot, realising that we were temporarily unarmed, began manoeuvring. He did tight spirals to avoid the incendiary and tracer bursts from the six machine guns of our adversaries that strafed the whole aircraft. With huge difficulty, known only to veterans, I was able to fix the jam, and shot at random to advise the pilot that the machine gun was working again.

'The pilot then straightened the aeroplane and dived desperately toward the lines. The attackers did the same, with lightning speed, chasing us and fanning us with bursts of fire. [I] defended desperately, but after about 50 shots the weapon jammed again. The pilot spiralled again. [I] was able again to fix the trouble amid incredible difficulties, given the strong wind and the centrifugal force of the aeroplane, which seemed to throw everything out. The pilot, realising that the weapon was again working, straightened up again and the aircraft resumed its perilous dive toward the lines with a dangerous manoeuvre. The defence was almost as desperate as the pilot's handling, but the attackers' machine guns stubbornly continued their inexorably destructive work.

'Eventually an enemy burst hit the observer's cockpit, breaking the clock and the windshield and piercing and splintering the camera. One more burst hit the pilot's seat, piercing the control wheel and smashing the altimeter and the RPM indicator – in fact all of the precision instruments. More bursts hit the engine, splintering the propeller, and the boiling water, spurting out violently, soaked the crew, making handling and defence very difficult.'

The front was by then not too distant, but a bullet hit the machine gun, silencing the weapon. The crew now had to rely exclusively on the pilot's flying abilities. However, 'the engine had a death rattle and the aeroplane, now falling to pieces, lost even more height. A sultriness,

**Fw Stefan Fejes in Albatros D III 153.29 of** *Flik* **51/J** *(Greg VanWyngarden)*

an unpleasant smell of fried oil due to the lack of water in the radiator and burnt struts hit by the incendiary bullets, induced fear of a fire'. In spite of this, the crew still tried to cross the frontline into friendly territory, but the aeroplane had by now lost so much height that it was skimming over a swamp. It was at this point that the fighters finally ceased firing.

Moments later the SAML S.2's undercarriage hit the surface of the water and the aircraft immediately capsized. Lioy and Montesi, almost unscathed, escaped from the wreck and were captured by soldiers who had arrived on the scene while the Italians were still wallowing ashore in a metre of muddy water. The crew met their victors, who praised them for their bravery and invited them to their mess, eventually also showing them their fighters, one of which had five bullet holes in it.

November ended for the Austro-Hungarian Albatros aces with one more 'victory', claimed on the 30th by Stojsavljevic near Monte Grappa. In his combat report he wrote;

'I took off this afternoon in response to an attack by enemy aircraft after hearing their engine noise. However, I reached a laggard when he was over Monte Peuma (height 1381 m), flying back to his lines. After about ten minutes of dogfighting in the area east of Monte Fontana Secca, I fired at a range of about 30 m (100 ft). A bullet from a well-aimed burst hit the water pipe of my aeroplane and, instantly enveloped in steam, I had to leave the fight. I am sure I hit him many times. I was not able to see what happened due to the vapour cloud (I shall claim a possible victory). This happened at 1430 hrs.'

The claim was eventually credited as a victory, but none of the intruders was shot down.

On 3 December Zgf Stefan Fejes was awarded his first confirmed victory with the D III – a *'draken'* – but this, the 26-year-old Hungarian-born pilot's sixth victory, remains unconfirmed in Allied documentation. According to a report quoted by O'Connor, Fejes was 'an earnest, modest, industrious and dependable flier. Speaks bad German. Good technical knowledge'. He had obtained all his previous victories with Brandenburg C Is of *Flik* 19. When war broke out Fejes had initially served in an infantry regiment, and with this unit he participated in the first battles on the Russian Front, but was severely wounded on 16 September 1914, less that two months after the start of hostilities. Following a long recuperation, Fejes was assigned to the motor service, then volunteered for aviation. After pilot training he was assigned to *Flik* 19 in Ajdussina on 3 February 1917, then moved to *Flik* 55 at the beginning of October that same year.

Two days later, on 5 December, Gräser was patrolling the area between Motta di Livenza, Treviso and the sea when he encountered a *39ª Squadriglia* Savoia-Pomilio engaged in a reconnaissance mission. Under the fire of the twin Schwarzlose M 16 machine guns of Albatros D III 153.44, the two-seater crashed near San Biagio. Although the aeroplane was destroyed, pilot Sergente Paolo Massagrande and observer Tenente Giuseppe Sproveri escaped unhurt.

On the ground, it now seemed that the worst was over for the Italians, allowing them to consolidate their defensive line. A reduction in Austro-Hungarian activity also allowed French and British troops to be deployed along the frontline – their transfer to Italy had been decided immediately after the Italian defeat at Caporetto. Hitherto, they had been kept in reserve in case of a breakthrough in the new line of defence.

The initial deployment of the VII Brigade of the Royal Flying Corps (RFC), which had arrived in Italy with the British XI and XIV Corps, included the 51st Wing with Royal Aircraft Factory RE 8s (Nos 34 and 42 Sqns), the 14th Wing with Sopwith Camels (Nos 28, 45 and 66 Sqns) and a Balloon Wing (the 4th, with the 9th and 20th Companies). The first flights in this new theatre of operations were flown from Grossa airfield, near Padua, on 29 November 1917 by RE 8s of Nos 28 and 34 Sqns.

On 7 December the Italian aviation command ordered a large attack in the area of Campomulo and Gallio that was to start at 1000 hrs and last until nightfall. This action would involve no fewer than 130 aircraft, including 30 from the French and British squadrons on the Italian Front. At 1100 hrs four SAML S.2s of *121ª Squadriglia* and three Savoia-Pomilios of *134ª Squadriglia* took off to bomb targets near Gallio and then strafe the enemy troops in the surrounding area. As they approached Gallio they met a formation of at least six fighters from *Flik* 55/J that had taken off from Pergine airfield and were patrolling from Asiago to Primolano.

Arigi, Kiss and Maier immediately shot down SAML S.2 3108, crewed by Caporale Pasquale Ceccarelli and Tenente Giuseppe Notarbartolo, who perished in the burning wreck. Then the Albatros attacked SAML S.2 3030 and riddled the aircraft with bullets, killing the observer, Tenente Edoardo Velo. The pilot, Tenente Pietro Giberti, was able to crash-land his aeroplane near San Giovanni, within the Italian lines. A third two-seater, piloted by Carabiniere Carlo Borello, and with Tenente Guido Cremano as observer, escaped and returned to its airfield without difficulty, despite its machine gun having jammed.

Almost at the same time a *134ª Squadriglia* patrol was attacked by Kenzian, Offz Stv Emanuel Stumpa and Kpl Gottlieb Munzar. Sottotenente Piero Baralis, piloting one of the Savoia-Pomilios, wrote the following account of the action in his combat report;

'While I was observing the effect of the bombs, which had created thick pillars of smoke and flames among the huts, I began to glide toward Gallio, where I had to strafe the area at the northern edge of the same village. I was attacked from the rear by three German aircraft. The first burst hit me in the left foot and the fight began, but I was able to escape, thanks especially to my gunner, Soldato Ferdinando Cantaluppi, who, with admirable calm, kept the three adversaries at bay with his machine gun, forcing one to retreat, probably hit.

'Just when I was outdistancing the enemy aircraft, a last burst fired from long range hit the engine, which immediately stopped. By juggling the throttle I was able to restart the engine and leave the enemy aeroplanes behind, chased by their final bursts of machine gun fire, and upon reaching Villaverla airfield I landed happily, with a bracing wire broken, the elevator very damaged and the aeroplane pierced in many parts (about 100 holes).'

Another Savoia-Pomilio, piloted by Tenente Laghi, made a precautionary landing in Villaverla with a damaged tail.

On 13 December the French *38º Compagnies d'Aerostiers* lost its first *'draken'* to enemy action when, near Meolo at about 1400 hrs, Brumowski, Linke-Crawford and Kaszala set the kite balloon ablaze. As usual there was strong anti-aircraft defence, and the rudder of Linke's Albatros D III was hit. After crossing the frontline the fighter crash-landed near Foca and turned over, but the pilot emerged from the wreckage unhurt. Brumowski recommended that Linke be awarded the *Goldene Tapferkeitmedaille* (Gold Bravery Medal) in the wake of this mission.

During a bombing raid against troops in Val Goccia on 16 December, an aeroplane of *115ª Squadriglia* fell to the fire of Kiss, Arigi and Lahner. After the raid the last SAML S.2 from a patrol of four aeroplanes inexplicably turned right instead of left and was cut off. Its escort, future aces Imolesi and Nicelli in two Nieuport 27s of *79ª Squadriglia*, saw the other S.2s turn towards the Italian lines and decided to follow the single machine, but they were bounced by the *Flik* 55/J flight, which attacked the two-seater. Nicelli and Imolesi tried to help, but they were so busy defending themselves that they could not stop the S.2 from being shot down in flames.

This action was watched from the ground by the parish priest of Seren del Grappa, Father Antonio Scopel, who wrote;

'After a long and hard battle in the sky of Monte Roncon, an Italian aeroplane, hit by incendiary bullets from an Austrian machine, came slowly down burning, slipped vertically in the air and came down near Caupo. When the machine landed, half-burnt Sergente Maggiore Motorista Fabbian Matteo from Borso leaned out from the aircraft, but he was dying. The other aviator, Tenente Orazio Giannini from Pistoia, fell from the aircraft into the river bed of the Torrente Stizzon, near the mill of Crudo. His body was utterly broken. The Austrians saw our aeroplane plunging down and shouted exultantly "Italianer kaputt, Italianer kaputt!"

Linke-Crawford poses boldly for a photograph that would be used in a series of propaganda images released by the Austro-Hungarians. The aeroplane is Albatros D III 153.16, which was the second aircraft to have the falcon on its fuselage sides. According to some sources its nose was painted red. On 13 December 1917 this fighter was hit during an attack against a French kite balloon, forcing Linke-Crawford to crash-land near Foca. The aircraft was repaired and then issued to a *Fliegerarsenal* test unit *(Koloman Mayrhofer)*

An official portrait of Oblt Benno Fiala von Fernbrugg. The medals on his tunic, all with *Kriegsdecoration und Schwertern* (War Decorations and Swords), are, from left to right, *Österreichisch-kaiserliche Leopolds-Orden* (Imperial Austrian Order of Leopold), *Österreichisch-kaiserliche Orden der eisernen Krone III Klass* (Imperial Austrian Order of the Iron Crown III Class), *Militärdienstkreuz III Klass* (Military Merit Cross) and *Militärverdienstmedaille* (Military Merit Medal). The ribbon on his chest denoted the German Iron Cross II Class, while under the breast pockets are the German and Austro-Hungarian pilot's badges *(Koloman Mayrhofer)*

'If these air battles in the clouds consisted only of manoeuvres they would be very entertaining to watch. But because one of the combatants has to suffer the fate of Icarus, one cannot smile at the manoeuvres, at the quick turns and movements and attacks. It is as bad as the terrible battles of the gladiators in ancient Roman arenas.'

A thick fog hampered aerial operations on 20 December, but Oblt Benno Fiala von Fernbrugg, flying Albatros D III 153.177, encountered an aeroplane identified as a 'Sopwith' and claimed to have brought it down near Monte Grappa, although such a loss is not recorded in Allied sources. Indeed, there are no reports of encounters with enemy aircraft on this date in RFC documentation, whereas the Italian records note several combats, so it is very probable that the Austro-Hungarian ace clashed with an Italian Hanriot HD.1 – an aircraft often mistaken for a Camel.

Fiala, born in Wien on 16 June 1890, was serving as technical officer with *Flik* 1 in Galicia when war broke out with Russia in August 1914, and he soon started flying as an observer – he also devised an effective radio set that was installed in aircraft within the unit. After moving to *Flik* 19 on the Isonzo Front in January 1916, Fiala was among the airmen who shot down Italian airship M.4 near Gorizia on 4 May. He was the observer in C I 61.55 on this occasion, the aircraft being flown by unit CO Hptm Ludwig Hautzmayer. Subsequently wounded in action, Fiala became a pilot after recovering from his injuries and, in June 1917, he was briefly posted to *Flik* 41/J, before moving on to *Flik* 12/D. With this unit, Fiala gained more confirmed victories flying the KD fighter, then joined *Flik* 56/J as deputy commander. This misidentified HD.1 was his 20th success, and his first with the Albatros D III.

Oblt Karl Patzelt achieved ace status on 29 December, flying a series 153 Albatros. During a fighter mission near the mouth of the Piave River, he claimed a Macchi L.3 of *252ª Squadriglia* from Venice, crewed by *2ª Capo Meccanico* Giorgio Parodi and Tenente Mario Morini. Although this was confirmed as Patzelt's fifth victory, the flying boat returned home with a number of bullet holes in it.

Patzelt, born in the Bohemian city of Crajowa in 1893, fought on the Russian Front in 1914 as a leutnant in *Schützen-Regiment Nr. 22*, being wounded for the first time on 21 November. Returning to the front with the rank of oberleutnant in March of the following year, he participated in the Gorlice–Tarnów Offensive, receiving several awards. However, Patzelt's health worsened and he was forced to take up duties in the rear from August 1915. In the spring of 1916 he was able to return to the front to lead a squad of assault troops, just in time to be involved in the bitter fighting that followed the Russian attack known as the Brusilov Offensive. On 16 June, 12 days after the start of the battle, he was wounded again, and during convalescence he decided to volunteer for the air service.

Patzelt's first aeronautical assignment was as technical officer of *Flik* 19 in Rumania, and he was soon flying missions as an observer. On 5 February 1917 he gained his first aerial victory in Brandenburg C I 26.44 piloted by StFw Andreas Dombrowski, claiming a Nieuport near Borsani. Patzelt was also taught to fly by Dombrowski, finishing his informal training in Italy, where he had been transferred to join *Flik* 34 in October 1917. Finally, he arrived at *Flik* 42/J, where he had the chance to fly fighters.

In front of a wall-mounted propeller and under the Christmas tree, NCO pilots of *Flik* 55/J celebrate the end of 1917 in Pergine, bearing a strange assortment of sparkling wine, dolls and a skull. They are, from left to right, unknown, Offz Stv Kiss, unknown, unknown, Fw Alois Lehmann, Kpl Franz Lahner and Kpl Munczar. The new year seemed so promising for the *LFT*, but some of these aviators did not survive to the end of 1918. Less than a month after this photograph was taken 'Josi' Kiss was shot down and severely wounded, and in May he was shot down again and killed. 'Lois' Lehmann was killed when he was shot down near Asiago on 23 April while flying D III 153.160, probably by Capt H B Bell of No 66 Sqn *(Bohumir Kudlicka)*

During the afternoon of the penultimate day of 1917, eight Caproni bombers, sent to attack the airfields in the area of San Fior di Sopra and Godega di San Urbano, clashed with a *Kette* of *Flik* 56/J led by Fiala. The deputy commander of the fighter unit, covered by Kpl Karl Haselböck, shot down Caproni Ca.4216 of *1ª Squadriglia* near Susegana. The entire crew – Capitano Maurizio Pagliano, Tenente Luigi Gori and gunners Arrigo Andri and Giovanni Caglio – lost their lives. Pagliano and Gori were combat veterans, and during previous months they had been accompanied by poet Gabriele d'Annunzio in their aeroplane on several missions. The Aviano military airport in Italy is now named after them.

The last Austro-Hungarian victory of the year was officially credited to Albatros pilot Oblt Gustav Edler von Salmon, who intercepted a reconnaissance aircraft and its five escort fighters at sunset near Noventa di Piave in D III 153.93 of *Flik* 41/J. The British aircraft that he claimed is not cited in Allied sources, however. The D III pilot suffered minor wounds to his hip and feet during the clash, forcing him to land on Motta di Livenza airfield. It seems that the RFC had no combats that afternoon, and Salmon's opponents could have been two Hanriot fighters of *82ª Squadriglia*, flown by Sergente Andrea Teobaldi and Soldato Clemente Panero.

Six days earlier, on Christmas Eve, Brumowski had left the front for well-deserved leave.

After some very bad moments during previous months, the Austro-Hungarian armed forces seemed to have ended the year on a triumphal note. The 'Russian bear' was out of the fight and was starting to tear itself to pieces in a bloody civil war, while the age-long Italian enemy seemed to be on the verge of collapse and about to suffer one more defeat to add to those already inflicted by the *K u K* army in the past. The Austrian writer Joseph Roth, lucid and bitter bard of the lost empire in his agonising years, would write in *The Emperor's Tomb*, 'Above the ebullient glasses from which we drank, invisible Death was already crossing his bony hands'. Those words fit perfectly the situation of the people and the army of the Hapsburg Empire at the beginning of 1918.

In Italy, recent defeats had given a burst of pride to the country and infused a new spirit in its soldiers, who now felt that they were struggling for national survival and the defence of their own homes. In response to the Italian plight the Allied powers sent not only military units but also an uninterrupted stream of material that replaced the equipment lost in the retreat, while industrial output in Italy itself was rising.

The situation on the other side of the front was quite different. Poor industrial planning, mistakes and the wastage of resources were combining with the lack of raw material reaching the Hapsburg Empire because of the Allied naval blockade to create a poisonous concoction that was shaking the nation and weakening its very foundations. The people started to suffer hunger, and soldiers and sailors watched events in Russia with increasing interest as nationalist ideas began to spread.

During January 1918 air superiority steadily passed back to the Italians and their allies. The threat was clearly seen by the *Armeeoberkommando*, which issued instructions to avoid the use of single aeroplanes in favour of mass deployment. However, it still hoped that 'through the creation of new units by all possible means, and the transfers of *Fliegerkompagnien* and *Ballonkompagnien* from the Russian to the Italian Front that have already begun, the above-mentioned balance of forces could be further improved in time for the start of fighting in the spring. Then, the superior quality of our flying personnel will ensure the attainment of air superiority. The number of British and French air units on the Italian Front is at least counterbalanced by the presence of German units'.

The ambitious military construction programmes not only failed to meet expectations, but also failed to make good the losses and attrition of war.

Kiss, Kenzian and Kasza obtained their first victory of the new year on 12 January when they combined to force RE 8 A4445 of No 42 Sqn to land near Asiago, behind Austro-Hungarian lines. Its crew, Lts G N Goldie and J D Barnes, were captured unscathed, having been prevented from burning their aircraft by Kiss – he had made a series of low passes at the RE 8 crew, simulating strafing runs. As usual, Goldie and Barnes were invited to Pergine before being sent to a prison camp.

On the 25th Lahner had a hard fight near Monte Lambara, and after crash-landing his damaged D III (153.70) he claimed a 'Nieuport single-seater'. His adversaries, however, were probably a patrol of Hanriots belonging to *81ª Squadriglia* and piloted by Tenente Giuseppe Lucci and Sergenti Alessandro Borgato and Ennio Sorrentino, all of whom returned safely to their airfield.

The next day Strohschneider and Gräser, who had transferred to *Flik* 61/J upon its activation at Motta di Livenza airfield, claimed a flying boat near Palude Maggiore, but there is no record of this loss. The aircraft was probably one of the Macchis from *252ª Squadriglia* that were involved in artillery spotting for Italian monitors. Similarly, the 'Sopwith' claimed by Kenzian is not listed in the Allied losses. That same day Kiss fought with a SAML S.2 of *115ª Squadriglia* near Monte Magnaboschi, claiming it as shot down. Although the aeroplane of pilot Capitano Ludovico Andreuzzi and observer Tenente Arnaldo Molaschi was damaged, it flew away.

This proved to be 'Josi' Kiss' last 'victory', for during the afternoon of the 27th he was severely wounded in the abdomen by the bullets fired either by Italian ace Capitano Antonio Riva or Sergente Maggiore

Adversaries, but members of the same exclusive club, Lts G N Goldie and J D Barnes fraternise with Kasza, Kenzian and Kiss, still partly in flying gear, who had shot them down on 12 January 1918. These men are, from left to right, Kasza, Goldie, Kenzian, Barnes, Kiss and Maier. The Albatros in the background, bearing a large black-and-white '7', is D III 153.47, the personal mount of Kiss, which also had a white band around the tail, just visible behind Maier's head *(Greg VanWyngarden)*

Gugliemo Fornagiari, both of *78ª Squadriglia*. Some previous authors have linked this action with the claim of 2Lt Matthew Brown Frew of No 28 Sqn RFC, but this does not match the facts. The British airman shot down his adversary in the morning, near Conegliano, which is far from the Asiago Plateau. Arigi told author Martin O'Connor that he hastened to the hospital where his friend had been taken after landing, only to find that Kiss remained untreated while the surgeon was eating!

In response to Arigi's angry words, the physician said he had to finish his meal, noting that the wounded pilot 'wasn't even an officer'. The strict class divisions of Austro-Hungarian society and the armed forces were a cancer that eventually contributed to the final collapse of the regime, but in this case Arigi's furious reaction forced the surgeon to do his duty.

Kiss survived, but his career as a fighter pilot was finished and he had to be moved away from the front. Following hospitalisation, he returned in May 1918 to *Flik* 55/J, when the unit was flying Phönix fighters. His new tour of duty was short and fruitless, Kiss being shot down and killed on 24 May when his D IIa, 422.10, crashed in a wood near Lamon following possible combat with Canadian ace 2Lt G A Birks of No 66 Sqn. Kiss had been almost obsessed by a desire to be an officer, but his dream came true too late, as he was posthumously promoted after his death – the only non-commissioned officer of the Austro-Hungarian Army to be so honoured. His Pergine girlfriend Erica Bonecker remained

Fw Josef Novak in front of his D III, 153.137, in January 1918. In addition to the name *Lil* on a black square, the aircraft also had the pilot's initials painted on the top wing. This Albatros, also used by Brumowski and Navratil, was lost on 6 May 1918 when Kpl Hans Schraffl was shot down and killed near Fossalta. Novak had gained two of his five victories (all claimed in C Is) as Brumowski's wingman on 17 July and 19 August 1917 *(Jiri Rajlich)*

With great skill and just as much luck, Hptm Godwin Brumowski was able to land and emerge unharmed from his battered D III 153.45, which had lost a good part of the fabric covering of its starboard wings in a fight with enemy fighters, probably British, on 1 February 1918. The extraordinary nature of the event seems to be reflected in the astonished attitude of the Austro-Hungarian soldiers gathered around the wreck *(Greg VanWyngarden)*

faithful to him, never married, and put flowers on the grave of her beloved 'Josi' until her own death.

In January, owing to illness, Arigi went to Aspern to act as a test pilot, but he would be back in action in Albania in the spring.

Nor was it a happy beginning of the new year for Brumowski, who was shot down twice in less that a week, on 1 and 4 February. He wrote to his friend Linke-Crawford;

'I just put my nose in this mess and those damned Englishmen shot me down twice. As you see, I'm not any better than you. On the first occasion I was alone against eight because the other knights had no will to fight, and I received 26 hits. Tank, wires and engine destroyed. The fight had been at an altitude of about 10-100 metres. Obviously the machine gun jammed.

'On the second occasion I was escorting a reconnaissance aircraft whose crew again had no eyes and did not see the approaching company. People watching from the ground counted 15-20 aeroplanes. Two or three persevered with Kaszala and the reconnaissance aeroplane, and the others with my red machine. This would not have mattered, but at 3000 m (9800 ft) the leading edge [of the wing] broke and all the fabric came away. This happened on the left side. The aeroplane began to turn around its horizontal axis, and the same thing happened on the right. I also noticed that the spar was broken. I said to myself, "Good night". I was still two kilometres (one mile) from the front.

'When the second wing also failed the aeroplane became easy to control, and I was able to cross the front, albeit by a hair's breadth, and crash-land. I capsized, but apart from that nothing happened. But I reprimanded my pilots. Only Kasza and Richter remained. I immediately dismissed five of the new ones.'

The harsh opinions voiced by some of the more battle-weary *Flik* pilots involved in these two clashes show the alarming state into which the *LFT* was sinking.

Brumowski's opponents on 1 February could have been five British Sopwith Camels of No 45 Sqn, which clashed with ten enemy aeroplanes, although they reported two 'indecisive encounters'. On 4 February Brumowski had to crash-land Albatros D III 153.52 near Passarella, along the Piave, and the only known possible candidates for this victory are two pilots from No 28 Sqn, who experienced combat between Mestre and Motta. Capt Jack Mitchell wrote in his combat report;

**Brumowski's opponents on 4 February could have been the No 28 Sqn Camels piloted by Capt Jack Mitchell and his very good friend 2Lt Percy Wilson. That day Mitchell was flying his favourite Camel, B6344 'G', seen here with a ribbon attached to an interplane strut and two mechanics wearing pith helmets** *(J A Brown via Andrew Kemp)*

'While on an offensive patrol at 15,000 ft Capt Mitchell saw AA shells bursting over Venice around three enemy aircraft at 10,000 ft. He attacked from the sun and got to within 80 yards [73 m] range of a yellow D III without being observed. He fired about 150 rounds into the enemy aircraft, which went down in a steep glide, crashed and burst into flames one kilometre south of Motta at

1005 hrs. A second enemy was claimed by 2Lt P Wilson, who attacked a red-striped D III and fired five rounds into him at 20 yards [18 m] range. The enemy aircraft glided down and crashed about six kilometres [four miles] west of Motta at about 1005 hrs.'

Although Motta is about 17 kilometres (ten miles) from the river, this was the only fight over that part of the front on 4 February, and the reference to a 'red-striped D III' seems significant.

Meanwhile, Strohschneider and Gräser had obtained their second confirmed victory flying *Flik* 61/J Albatros fighters on 30 January, when, according to an Intelligence Summary of the RFC in Italy, 'one machine of No 34 Sqn was attacked by five Albatros Scouts and shot down in flames just east of Nervesa'. Lts R S Gaisford and L W B Moore lost their lives in the wreck of RE 8 B6487, and they now rest in the British War Cemetery at Tezze.

Whilst patrolling over the Plateau at 1130 hrs on 21 February, Lahner, flying D III 153.158, attacked an Italian SP.2 two-seater from *33ª Squadriglia* that fired back. He was then obliged to defend himself against the escorting fighter, a *78ª Squadriglia* Hanriot piloted by ace 'Fo-Fo' Fornagiari, who hit the Albatros and forced Lahner to land near Asiago, where his aircraft was quickly destroyed by Italian artillery shells. The SP.2 crew of Capitano Casimiro Fusco and observer Tenente Giuseppe Calì returned to base and credited Fornagiari with his seventh victory, while the *LFT* awarded the Savoia-Pomilio to Lahner as his fifth!

That same day, along the Piave River, a *Kette* of *Flik* 51/J led by the unit's commanding officer, Fiala, clashed with a patrol from No 66 Sqn

**Luck again smiled on Brumowski on 4 February, when he was able to limp across the lines in his badly damaged D III 153.52 and crash-land on a grassy field near Passarella. Although the aeroplane was a total loss, being formally written off in June, the ace left the cockpit without a scratch. The wheel discs show the black-and-yellow colours introduced as *Flik* markings in October 1917 and used for a brief period (*Rudi Höfling*)**

**Zgf Jan Skvor in front of Albatros D III 53.46 of *Flik* 27/D on Ora airfield. This aircraft was destroyed in a crash on 25 February 1918, its pilot, Hptm Johann Frint, who was performing aerobatics at the time, being killed. Frint had previously served as observer in *Flik* 23 prior to being trained as a pilot (*Boris Ciglic*)**

RFC in the region of Isola Papadopoli. Fiala, in D III 153.128, claimed a Camel, and so did Tahy and Kasza near Cascina Zonta, a few kilometres east of Maserada.

On 24 February 2° Capo Macchinista Giorgio Parodi was wounded in the right leg in a fight with Strohschneider, Gräser, Ltn Edgar Mörath and Ltn Otto Schrimpl, who claimed a 'Wasser Nieuport' in the Venetian lagoon, but Macchi M.5 M 7102 alighted with no further damage and was towed back to Venice.

On 8 March Gräser, Mörath and Schrimpl attacked a kite balloon near the mouth of the Piave, and although its envelope was riddled with bullets, the balloon, No 60, did not catch fire. The previous day a flying accident had resulted in the death of Oblt Alexander Tahy. His D III, 153.69, crashed shortly after taking off from Mansuè airfield, probably due to wing failure. Tahy, who had eight confirmed victories to his name (five of which were obtained flying two-seaters), was attempting to fly his 100th combat mission when he was killed.

Born in Nyiregyhaza, Hungary, Tahy was a career artillery officer who had joined the *LFT* in 1916. His first victory, Caproni Ca.1233 of *1ᵃ Squadriglia*, which he shared with Brumowski, Lschlt Gottfried Banfield and several other Austro-Hungarian airmen, was gained from the observer's seat of Brandenburg C I 20.08, piloted by Fw Heinrich Mahner. During this combat Tahy was slightly wounded by a bullet fired from the bomber.

At dawn on 12 March 1918 Albatros fighters of *Flik* 51/J and 61/J attacked Marcon airfield with bombs and machine gun fire but did little damage. On the way home Gräser and Schrimpl claimed an SVA near Monastier, although according to Italian sources the only event that matches this claim is a forced landing by Italian ace Ancillotto due to engine trouble.

Eight days later Strohschneider led five aeroplanes of *Flik* 61/J that were armed with ten small bombs in a night attack on Italian positions near Zenson. While landing his Phönix D I, 228.36, Strohschneider crashed and was killed. The ace had claimed his 15th, and final, victory on 16 March, sharing it, as usual, with Gräser.

On 22 March Tenente Ferruccio Marzari of *3ᵃ Sezione SVA* was engaged in a reconnaissance flight between Vittorio Veneto and Sacile when he was suddenly attacked by enemy aircraft, although he managed to escape. The Italian pilot become the second 'victory' of Fw Stefan Fejes and the first for Zgf Karl (or Dragutin) Balzareno of *Flik* 51/J. The following day SAML S.2 2540 of *39ᵃ Squadriglia* was on its way to Tessera airfield when the crew decided to head back over the frontline, perhaps to take more photographs. Invisible against the cloudy sky was a patrol of *Flik* 61/J aircraft, which encircled the two-seater over Romanziol. The S.2 pilot tried to dive, but the aircraft was shot down in flames by Gräser, killing Sergente Achille Zardi and Tenente Amedeo Busseti.

For an account of the events on 30 March 1918, which led to the award of the Victoria Cross to Lt Alan Jerrard of No 66 Sqn, we can quote the words of Fiala, who in 1964 told the story in a letter to Norman Macmillan, author of the book *Offensive Patrol* and a former pilot on the Italian Front. That morning Jerrard was with Lt Harold R Eycott-Martin in a patrol led by Capt Peter Carpenter that fought with a *Kette* of Albatros D IIIs from *Flik* 51/J. Fiala recalled;

'At about midday on a clear and sunny day, I was coming back to my airfield at the head of my patrol of four following an uneventful escort flight of one hour and ten minutes for a photo-reconnaissance aeroplane of *Flik 32*. We arrived at our airfield of Ghirano at a height of about 1400 m [4500 ft], and as I flew over its northern corner three Camels attacked us from the southwest, diving out of the sun

from a considerable height. I saw far ahead of me an NCO pilot turn and fight with Camel Nº 1 [Jerrard]. A second Camel [Nº 2] then came at me from above. He was higher than me, so I climbed and hit him from beneath. Camel Nº 2 was also attacked from behind by my squadron companion, Fw Fejes, who pushed it toward the ground, and the Piave River, with his machine gun fire.

'Because of this I turned to the right with a 180-degree right spiral turn and put myself on course 230. I then saw Camel Nº 1 in front of me on course 50. We flew one against the other at an altitude of about 1200 m [3900 ft]. From a distance of about 1000 m [1100 yards] I fired about 100 shots, and saw the phosphorous bullets explode as they hit the Camel's Ruston-Clerget engine. Its pilot, Lt Jerrard, probably surprised and shocked by the well-aimed hits on his engine, dived, and I followed him, just passing over the Camel in a diving turn of 140 degrees at full throttle. I then had the Camel [Jerrard] in front of me at lower height, and after a right turn of 140 degrees it was on course 190 degrees, heading toward the Piave. I fired about 100 rounds from 500-300 m [550-330 yards], while above me my squadronmate, Bönsch, also fired on the Camel. He stopped firing, like me, when he saw that the fighter's propeller had stopped.'

The Camel crash-landed in grass about four kilometres (2.5 miles) from the airfield, cutting down a willow tree and breaking its fuselage. It was soon encircled by soldiers. Fifteen minutes later Fiala arrived in a car to find the British pilot stunned but unscathed. Jerrard was later driven to the same hospital where Capt Kenneth B Montgomey of No 66 Sqn had been taken following his capture on 22 February. According to Fiala some listening devices were hidden in their room, but the British officers preferred to speak about pretty nurses rather than military secrets.

In his letter to Macmillan, Fiala also revealed the secret of his luck. He had painted a black 'Drudenfuss' onto his D III, 153.155, this five-pointed star motif, according to Tyrolean folklore (Fiala's family originated from Valsugana), affording protection from witches and, it appears, enemy bullets too!

The text of the citation for Jerrard's Victoria Cross stated;

'When on an offensive patrol with two other officers he attacked five enemy aeroplanes and shot one down in flames, following it down to within 100 ft of the ground.

The darkened wing insignia uniquely applied to RFC aircraft in Italy is shown to advantage in this photograph of smashed Camel B5648 'E' of Lt Alan Jerrard in a field about four kilometres from Ghirano airfield, where it crashed on 30 March 1918 after a fight with Oblt Benno Fiala von Fernbrugg of *Flik* 56/J. The soldiers on the right are standing around the British pilot, whom they have just pulled from the wreck (*Author's collection*)

Unscathed but in shock, Jerrard sits on the trunk of the willow tree uprooted by his aircraft. He later told author, and fellow pilot, Norman Macmillan 'I was bloody lucky to be a prisoner'. He was the only Camel pilot to receive the Victoria Cross, given to him on 5 April 1919 by King George V at Buckingham Palace (*Author's collection*)

Zgf Eugen Bönsch of *Flik* 51/J flew Albatros D III 153.140 in the spring of 1918. In this aircraft he participated in an attack on the Italian airfield at Marcon on 12 March. It is interesting to note how the raiders were seen by ground observers, the Italian Headquarters Daily Report of the following day stating, 'Yesterday at dawn two enemy aircraft without the usual identification markings but with white discs on the fuselage came down at very low level over Marcon airfield, dropping some bombs and strafing. No damage, no victims. A cruising patrol of our aeroplanes mistook them for friendly aircraft and did not intervene because the anti-aircraft artillery did not fire' *(Jiri Rajlich)*

On Gajarine airfield *Flik* 69/S armourers fuse bombs for the next mission under the watchful eyes of the Brandenburg C I's crew. By the summer of 1918 Italian and Allied aircraft had gained total air superiority, making it almost impossible for *LFT* fighters to fulfil their escort duties for highly vulnerable aeroplanes such as these *(Boris Ciglic)*

'He then attacked an enemy aerodrome from a height of only 50 ft from the ground, and, engaging single-handed some 19 machines, which were either landing or attempting to takeoff, succeeded in destroying one of them, which crashed on the aerodrome. A large number of machines then attacked him, and whilst thus fully occupied he observed that one of the pilots of his patrol was in difficulties. He went immediately to his assistance, regardless of his own personal safety, and destroyed a third enemy machine.

'Fresh enemy aeroplanes continued to rise from the aerodrome, which he attacked one after another, and he only retreated, still engaged with five enemy machines, when ordered to do so by his patrol leader. Although apparently wounded, this very gallant officer turned repeatedly and attacked single-handed the pursuing machines until he was eventually overwhelmed by numbers and driven to the ground.

'Lt Jerrard had greatly distinguished himself on four previous occasions, within a period of 23 days, in destroying enemy machines, displaying bravery and ability of the very highest order.'

During this combat, Fejes, who had claimed a Camel destroyed near the Piave, was forced to land on Ghirano airfield owing to a pierced water pipe.

On 3 April Bönsch claimed a *'draken'* near San Biagio – probably one of the balloons belonging to $3^a$ or $10^a$ *Sezione* that was attacked that day without serious damage being inflicted.

It is difficult to reconstruct the details of the events of 17 April, which was a hectic and bloody day. Two *Kette* of *Flik* 42/J took off to escort a Brandenburg C I of *Flik* 53/D that was to direct artillery fire. On its way back home the formation was bounced by a large patrol of Italian Hanriots, identified as 'Sopwiths' by the Austro-Hungarian pilots. Oblt Michael Gassner-Nordon von Laudon was attacked

73

first, and when he tried to escape by diving, the wings of his D III, 153.152, failed and the aeroplane crashed near Bigolino, killing him. Seeking to avenge Laudon's loss, Ltn Ladislaus Ujvari and StFw Johann Riszticz claimed a fighter, while Udvardy and Fw Franz Oberst tried to protect Brandenburg C I 169.35. In spite of their efforts the two-seater was hit and shed its wings, crashing near Valdobbiadene.

The ordeal was not yet over, however, because immediately after the C I's demise, the Albatros flown by Oblt Richard Fitz, in the second *Kette*, was hit, although he was able to make it back to his airfield.

One victory was officially credited to Ujvari, Riszticz, Fw Ferdinand Takacs and StFw Friedrich Hefty. The last-named pilot, born in Bratislava on 13 December 1894, had left school before graduation to follow his passion for aviation – a decision that, as with Kiss, prevented him achieving coveted officer status. His first frontline assignment was to *Flik* 12 just after Italy entered the war, but he was wounded in the foot by ground fire on 7 October 1915. After a stint as a test pilot in Aspern and more tours of duty flying two-seaters on the Italian and Rumanian fronts, Hefty joined *Flik* 42/J with one confirmed victory, claiming his second on 27 October 1917 flying Aviatik D I 38.10.

The Italians actually suffered no losses during the combat of 17 April 1918, but it is possible that 2Lt William George Hargrave of No 28 Sqn perished in this encounter, shot down over Montello in Camel B6342. The other possible adversaries of the British pilot are Brumowski and Navratil, but it seems more probable that they clashed with a patrol from *91ª Squadriglia* in a different dogfight. Their claim over Arcade matches the report by Sergente Guido Nardini, who stated that he had engaged a red fighter.

That same day Ltn Franz Rudorfer and Ltn Bönsch believed that they had shot down SIA.7b 8329 of *27ª Squadriglia*. Although it had indeed been hit 20 times and subsequently written off, the biplane was able to return to its airfield. The crew, Sergente Pio Alessandrini and Capitano Armando Del Sole, emerged from their ordeal unscathed, in spite of a bullet being stopped by the officer's seat-belt buckle.

On 1 May Fw Fejes had a fight with a 'Sopwith one-seater' and claimed it near Breda di Piave, receiving confirmation from *58 Infanteriedivision* and *XVI Korpskommando*. That same day Fiala received confirmation for four victories – three aeroplanes and a kite balloon – during two different missions, but these alleged successes do not tally with known Allied losses.

On 4 May Patzelt and three wingmen of *Flik* 68/J became involved in a melée with Camels of No 66 Sqn, the RFC aircraft soon being joined by fighters from Nos 28 and 45 Sqs and the Italian ace Sergente Nicelli. During the course

Pergine, 10 May 1918, and *Flik* 55 airmen gather around a D III marked 'K'. In the front row, from left to right, are Kpl Otto Kullas, Zgf Wilhelm Holzer and Kpl Franz Pelzmann. In the second row, again from left to right, are Oblt Hans Leiner and Ltns Anton Schamburek, von Maier, Kiss, Kenzian and Behounek. Lahner is seated on the propeller, while Oblt Karl Princig Ritter von Hervalt is perched on the top wing and Kasza stands on the lower wing. The aircraft is probably D III 153.186 *(Jiri Rajlich)*

**The remains of Albatros D III 153.221, in which Ltn Franz Gräser was shot down and killed on 17 May 1918, lie alongside a dirt road near Pero, on the Italian bank of the Piave** *(Aeronautica Militare Italiana)*

of the engagement Patzelt and Kpl Karl Fritsch were shot down and killed, while StFw Andreas Dombrowski, in D III 153.195, was slightly wounded in the face and forced to land. There were no known losses on the Allied side, although victories were confirmed for *Flik* 68/J pilots (two to Fritsch and one to Dombrowski). This was the sixth, and last, 'victory' for Dombrowski – and his only success with the Albatros D III – and it earned him the *Silberne Tapfekeitmedaille 1. Klasse.*

Born of German parents in Märisch-Ostrau (now in the Czech Republic), Dombrowski was drafted into the army at the outbreak of war, receiving Austro-Hungarian Pilot's Certificate No 382 on 17 June 1916. Prior to being transferred to the Italian front to join *Flik* 68/J in April 1918, he had gained a remarkable reputation as a two-seater pilot on the Russian Front, with five confirmed victories. Following convalescence for the wounds he received on 4 May fighting the British Camels, Dombrowski swapped fighters for reconnaissance aircraft and continued to fly these machines until war's end.

That spring, with preparations for the next Austro-Hungarian offensive in full swing, the *LFT* was tasked with conducting myriad reconnaissance flights beyond enemy lines that cost it dearly in men and materiel owing to ever-increasing Allied air superiority on the Italian front.

On 17 May a *Flik* 61/J patrol led by Gräser escorted Brandenburg C I 229.30 of *Flik* 12/Rb on just such a photo-reconnaissance flight. Near San Biagio they were bounced by Italian fighters, the Austro-Hungarian formation leader being attacked by Tenente Gastone Novelli and Sergente Cesare Magistrini. As Gräser tried to escape in a dive, Sergente Guido Nardini, who was flying some 200 m (650 ft) lower than his comrades, immediately attacked the Albatros and sent it crashing in flames near Pero. The victory was officially credited to all three Italian aces. Gräser's body was recovered from the charred remains of his D III, 153.221, and buried in a grave that has never been traced.

Five days later a *Kette* from *Flik* 51/J was tasked with escorting Brandenburg C I 369.30 of *Flik* 19/D. As they approached the Piave River the patrol was attacked from above by SPADs flown by ranking Italian ace Francesco Baracca and his wingman Sergente D'Urso. The former set ablaze D III 153.155, piloted by Fähnrich Ernst Pontalti, which crashed, killing the South Tyrolean pilot. This was Baracca's 32nd success. Fejes in turn claimed one of the SPADs, but both Italian fighters returned safely to Quinto di Treviso airfield.

On 26 May nine D IIIs of *Flik* 42/J took off to escort a *Flik* 57/Rb photographic aircraft well within Italian territory. Three of the fighters were forced to abandon the mission and the remainder were attacked between Treviso and the Piave River by a multitude of aircraft – at least three *91$^a$ Squadriglia* SPADs, three No 28 Sqn Camels, two *78$^a$*

*Squadriglia* Hanriots and, probably, another Hanriot of *76ª Squadriglia*, piloted by Italian ace Flavio Torello Baracchini.

Zgf Franz Hofstätter, who had become slightly separated from the patrol, was shot down in flames in the initial stages of the combat, and the formation was then thrown into disorder when the pilots tried to escape by diving. Udvardy was able to crash-land his aeroplane, while Ujvari was chased for a long time and nearly forced to do the same. He was ultimately saved by ground fire that drove away two fighters, allowing him to crash-land on his airfield. A shared victory that is non-existent in Allied records was assigned to Ujvari, who had been a mechanical engineering student before the war, and Zgf Anton Aussitz.

On 6 June Fiala claimed two confirmed victories in two different missions (one at about midday and the other at 1900 hrs) that do not match any recorded Allied losses. The second claim refers to a brief combat with two *81ª Squadriglia* fighters that had to leave the fight owing to their machine guns jamming.

Fate summoned Ludwig Telessy on the morning of 9 June 1918. He was engaged with other pilots of *Flik* 9/J in escorting Phönix 121.20 of *Flik* 15/F when the Austro-Hungarian patrol was attacked by Camels of No 66 Sqn. Telessy was severely wounded by bullets fired by Canadian ace Capt William Barker and 2Lt G A Birks, and had to crash-land Albatros D III 153.51 near Marter, in Val Sugana. He was taken to hospital but succumbed to his wounds the following day. Buried in the cemetery at Levico, Telessy was posthumously awarded the *Goldene Tapferkeitsmedaille* for the second time.

On 15 June the last Austro-Hungarian offensive was launched, and from dawn airmen of the *LFT* were in action directly above the battlefield. They quickly encountered tough opposition that mowed them down. On the ground, however, the *K u K* regiments were able to create two dangerous bridgeheads on the west bank of the Piave in the Montello and Zenson areas.

The second day of the *LFT* campaign saw attacks against Allied kite balloons, which were directing artillery fire on *K u K* gathering points and the temporary bridges built across the Piave. Brumowski and a wingman flamed the *'draken'* of *7ª Sezione* at about 1700 hrs, forcing its occupants to take to their parachutes. Meanwhile, Bönsch claimed a balloon of *11ª Sezione* that was saved by the quick reaction of the winch crew and furious ground fire, although observer Tenente Aldo Urbani suffered a leg wound.

On the 17th Fiala, flying D III 153.270, was engaged in low-level strafing of the enemy trenches near Fossalta when two bullets hit his left wrist. He flew back to his airfield, had the wound bandaged and returned to the fight.

After their initial successes the Austro-Hungarian troops were stopped in their tracks, but the final outcome of the offensive remained in the balance, with furious attacks and counterattacks continuing.

On 19 June Brumowski, with Oblt Rupert Terk of *Flik* 63/J, destroyed the *'draken'* of *55ª Sezione* near the Italian coastline, and again the observer descended by parachute. The leading Austro-Hungarian ace then attacked SAML S.2 3110 of *39ª Squadriglia*, which was strafing troops south of Zenson. He duly shot the biplane down in flames, killing the crew, Tenenti Carlo Scavini and Mario Beltramolli.

Delivered in February 1918, Albatros D III 153.169 was assigned to Flik 42/J, where it was flown by StFw Friedrich Hefty from April to June 1918. This pilot gained three victories with the aircraft, which is seen here with fellow ace Oblt Franz Rudorfer. As these photographs show, the aircraft had different markings on either side of its fuselage *(Greg VanWyngarden)*

That same day over Falzé di Piave, SP.3 6732 of *23ª Squadriglia* was dropping its bombs when it was attacked by a single-seater. Observer Sottotenente Giovanni Borreani released the last three bombs while his pilot, Sottotenente Bellini, dived toward Nervesa. The fighter's bullets hit the Italian aeroplane repeatedly, but luckily Sergente Oreste Codeghini of *78ª Squadriglia* was in the vicinity in his Hanriot, and he drove away the fighter while the SP.3 crash-landed near Volpago. The only possible candidate for this victory seems to be Fiala, but according to the available sources he claimed his prey near San Biagio di Collalta – some distance away from the area in which the aeroplane of *23ª Squadriglia* was attacked.

It is difficult to reconstruct what happened over Montello on 20 June because there were many dogfights taking place at roughly the same time (from 1040 hrs to 1100 hrs), with a number of aircraft and units involved. Allied aircraft that definitely engaged *Flik* 42/J, 51/J and 61/J were fighters from *78ª* and *81ª Squadriglie*, SIA.7b reconnaissance aeroplanes of *22ª*, *36ª* and *48ª Squadriglie* and single Camels from Nos 28 (flown by ace Lt A G Cooper) and 45 Sqns (with American ace Lt C G Catto at the controls).

Following this clash, officially confirmed victories were accredited to Sergente Alfio Lepore and Tenente Lodi (the crew of an SIA.7b of *22ª Squadriglia*), Sergente Rennella (*78ª Squadriglia*), Tenente Brenta and Sergente Codeghini (*78ª Squadriglia*). The latter two aviators were awarded two victories each, these probably being shared with the above-mentioned British pilots. In reality, the only known *LFT* loss was Offz Stv Friedrich Hefty of *Flik* 42/J, who landed at Pianzano airfield in his damaged D III 153.169.

Austro-Hungarian airmen were awarded a total of 11 victories – Fiala claimed three, Hefty two and Brumowski, Bönsch, Udvardy, Oblt Friedrich Dechant, Fw Josef Proksch and Zgf Ludwig Deubler one each. The Allied losses were Sergente Antonio Nava, killed in his *81ª Squadriglia* Hanriot, and Sergente Piero Palesa, killed with Tenente Giovanni Solenghi in a SIA.7b of *36ª Squadriglia*. Only the opponent of Brumowski is known for certain – the SIA.7b of Tenenti Arturo Scanavino and Benigno Donadoni of *48ª Squadriglia*. The former wrote in his logbook;

'Bombed and strafed enemy troops with Ten Oss B Donadoni in the area Montello-Falzé di Piave. Dropped 18 bombs and fired 50 machine gun shots. Attacked over San Croce by an enemy fighter, and unable to defend due to jammed machine guns, I put the aeroplane in a glide with the engine at 800 rpm to return to the airfield. Donadoni screamed "There is the Austrian!", then with presence of mind he brought his gun to bear, but unfortunately it didn't work!

Groundcrew work on Albatros D III 153.209, the last aeroplane flown in combat by Brumowski during World War 1. The ace obtained his last victory whilst flying this fighter when, on 20 June, he downed an Italian SIA.7b that flipped over onto its back when it landed on Istrana airfield. A mounting for a flare gun can be seen fitted on the Albatros' upper wing centre section *(Jiri Rajlich)*

'The red D III, knowing it was impossible to reach us, did an about-turn while three of our fighters crossed the lines and perhaps attacked it. During the volleys fired at us, one explosive bullet burst near me. Fearing the radiator had been pierced I landed on Istrana airfield, but the left wheel had been holed by three bullets and the aeroplane slewed round and turned over – the observer and I were unscathed, but the aeroplane was unusable.

'We found that our adversary had aimed well because he pierced the tyre of the left wheel three times, put one bullet in the upper wing and three in the left lower wing, one in the right lower wing, one in the rudder and one in the fuselage, which entered under the seats of myself and the observer. That evening in the mess we had to pay for Champagne.'

When the sun rose on the Piave on the morning of 24 June, Austro-Hungarian troops had retreated from the western bank of the river in the Montello sector, and with them went their last hope of reversing the tide and winning the war. Air superiority had been a key element in the Italian victory. The losses suffered by the *LFT* during the offensive, known in Italy as the 'Solstice Battle', were so terrible that Austro-Hungarian airmen called this period 'The Black Weeks'. According to a recent Austrian study, from 15 to 24 June 1918 the *Isonzoarmee* alone lost 22 per cent of its pilots, 19 per cent of its observers and 41 per cent of its aeroplanes.

Neither the *LFT* nor the Hapsburg Army ever recovered from this blow, their effectiveness being slowly strangled by ever worsening shortages of almost everything. The Austro-Hungarians had a desperate requirement for men and supplies in the frontline that could not be fulfilled because they simply did not exist. From the beginning of the war, local aviation manufacturers had wasted already scarce resources on ill-conceived

Fighters of *Flik* 3/J on Romagnano airfield during the last summer of the war. On the right are the aircraft of Oblt Stefan Stec (153.234, identified by a horizontal 'S') and Oblt Friedrich Navratil (253.06, with a heart pierced by an arrow). The pilots of this unit received confirmation for 12 victories from July 1918 to war's end. Five casualties were suffered in the same period *(Aeronautica Militare Italiana)*

*Flik* 3/J's Oblt Stec also had his insignia applied to 253.117, which was delivered in early August 1918 and had only a short life with the unit because it crashed on the airfield during a training flight on the 18th of that same month, killing Oblt Ernst Herold von Stoda *(Aeronautica Militare Italiana)*

Oblt Franz Rudorfer volunteered in 1915 and initially served in *Infanterieregiment* 59, moving to the air service in July 1917. Assigned to *Flik* 51/J in April 1918, he gained 12 aerial victories before war's end. Rudorfer died on 13 November 1919, aged just 22 *(Greg VanWyngarden)*

projects, and they now lacked the skilled workers and raw materials to build new aeroplanes. They were also unable to send spare parts, fuel and even paint and bracing wires to the front. This left Austro-Hungarian airmen with little option but to bear their pain and continue to fight and die without hope, fully aware of the futility of their sacrifice.

On 25 June, when Brumowski left the command of *Flik* 41/J for thee months' leave, he had 439 combat missions recorded in his logbook. He returned to the front in October as commanding officer of the *Isonzoarmee* fighter groups, but no more missions were recorded.

In the weeks after the final Battle of Piave, Navratil became an ace, claiming three victories between 16 and 23 July. On the 16th he was leading a *Flik* 3/J *Kette* near Lake Garda when it came under attack from a patrol of Italian Hanriot fighters. Navratil and StFw Otto Förster received confirmation of two victories apiece, while future ace Oblt Franz Peter and Oblt Stefan Stec were credited with downing one aeroplane each. The only known Italian loss was Tenente Amerigo Crocetti, who landed on Lodrone airfield wounded in the foot by an incendiary bullet. Navratil was flying Albatros D III 253.06, and his were the first confirmed victories using a series 253 aeroplane.

There are fewer doubts about his sixth victory, claimed on 23 July. Bristol F 2B Fighter C4759 of No 139 Sqn was shot down in flames near Mattarello Railway Station, its crew, 1Lt William Lennox Vorster and Sgt Herbert George Frow, perishing. Both men were buried in a grave that still exists in the local cemetery. Franz Peter was born in Wien on 8 October 1896, and after a period as an observer he qualified as a pilot in March 1918.

Seven days later, on 30 July, another F 2B from the same unit was claimed by Fiala near Passarella di Sotto. Fiala and his wingmen were escorting a reconnaissance aeroplane of *Flik* 34/D that was to direct the artillery fire of *XXIII Korps* when they were attacked by a No 139 Sqn patrol led by future Australian ace Capt Sydney Dalrymple. The F 2Bs dived on the enemy fighters below, and future ace Lt Walter C Simon, an American pilot flying C999 with Lt William W Smith, fired at a D III. Then, after a right-hand climbing turn, he sent a 100-round burst into another fighter. In the following melée Smith was wounded in the foot by a bullet, but the crew claimed three more enemy aeroplanes before the engagement ended. All five claims were officially confirmed, and Simon received the Distinguished Flying Cross. The Austro-Hungarian formation suffered no losses, however. For their part, Fiala and Rudorfer were credited with two equally non-existent victories.

That evening at about 1900 hrs, a *23ª Squadriglia* crew saw an aeroplane spin out of a dark cloud and crash on the Montello. Savoia-Pomilio SP.2 7813, in which Caporale Giuseppe Boccioni and Tenente Vito Simoncelli perished, was lost due to unknown causes according to Italian sources, but on this date a two-seater was claimed by Mörath.

On 4 August Sergente Giovanni Arrigoni, an expert pilot with four victories to his name, flew SVA 5 11850 to Romagnano Airfield for a photographic mission. He was shot down near Aldeno by D III 253.05, flown by Peter, who, according to a testimony, later attended the burial dressed in a white uniform. The SVA wreck was given the identifying number 76 by the *Evidenz und Kontroll Gruppe*.

On 5 August SAML S.2 3080 of *121ª Squadriglia* fell near Mattarello to Navratil while it was flying a reconnaissance mission between Mori and Calliano, on the right bank of the Adige River. When, at war's end, the Italians found the graves of Vicebrigadiere Carlo Borello and Tenente Luigi Franchi, some of the wreath laid by the Austro-Hungarian troops still remained, with a tribute to the fallen adversaries on the ribbon.

Three days later Bönsch set ablaze a *'draken'* of *11ª Sezione* during an evening patrol, its observers jumping out. An Italian artillery officer saw the action and wrote the following account in his diary;

'Slipping silently between the sunset red clouds he came near it, fired the deadly rocket and came away at enormous speed, vainly pursued by the anti-aircraft fire.'

Navratil gained one more victory on the 16th, when his *Kette* attacked a patrol of F 2Bs from No 139 Sqn near Trento. During the encounter D8069 crashed, killing Lt Cyril R H Jackson and 2Lt William F Keepin.

On 22 August, on the Piave Front, Italian ace Capitano Bartolomeo Costantini saw flames burst from the Albatros on which he was firing. Almost immediately the pilot jumped from the cockpit, a grim but not unusual sight under such circumstances, but this time Costantini was astonished to see a parachute open. As noted by the *91ª Squadriglia* war diary, 'It was the first time that a parachute had been put to practical use in an aircraft'. The lucky pilot was Hefty, the five-victory ace barely being able to leave his doomed D III, 253.71. Although he suffered a sprained ankle when he landed, Hefty's parachute had saved his life. Delivery of German Heinecke Sitzpolster parachutes had commenced earlier that

A signed portrait of Oblt Friedrich Navratil. His ten confirmed victories were all obtained flying the Albatros D III *(Koloman Mayrhofer)*

Navratil's ninth victim, Bristol F 2B Fighter D7966 'A' of No 139 Sqn, was forced to crash-land on Gardolo airfield on 23 August 1918. Its crew, Lts C E Gill and T Newey, were captured unharmed *(Jiri Rajlich)*

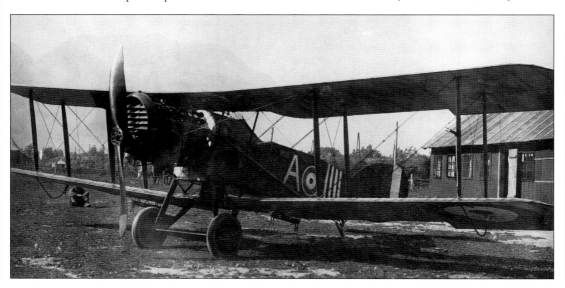

A white four-leafed clover on a black square identified Albatros D III 153.199 of *Flik* 3/J. This was the insignia of StFw Otto Förster, but Navratil and Kpl August Korkish also flew the aircraft. It is known that 153.199 suffered a minor accident on Romagnano airfield during the summer of 1918 *(Jiri Rajlich)*

On 23 September 1918 a hurricane struck the Venetian plain, sweeping aside aircraft and hangars. The wind upturned and destroyed D III 153.144 of *Flik* 61/J, which in February had belonged to *Flik* 61/J and been flown by Gräser *(Ivo Michael Forti)*

month, but the pilots generally distrusted them, and they were also cumbersome and uncomfortable to wear.

An F 2B of No 139 Sqn was forced to land on Gardolo airfield by Navratil on the 23rd, and Lts C E Gill and T Newey became unintentional guests of the *Kaiser*. That same day a *Flik* 3/J patrol clashed with some more F 2Bs, and D7966 received a bullet in the engine and was forced to land on Gardolo airfield. The enemy aircraft's approach in a steep dive was mistaken by ground personnel, who, fearing a strafe, scattered everywhere. They were reassured only by the intervention of the commanding officer of *Flik* 10/F, Oblt Otto Wehofer, the technical officer of *Flik* 27/F, Ltn Friedrich Teimer, and a mechanic from the same unit, Fw Hyrek. Teimer and Hyrek were quick to reach the British aeroplane, extinguishing the fire started by the now captive crew. This gallant act was praised by the Command of the 10th Army, and the aircraft was transported to *Fliegerarsenal* and given the number 83. In October 1918 it was written off for an unknown reason.

During the first two weeks of September Mörath obtained his last two victories, sharing them with Fw Robert Grabenhofer. On 7 September the pair claimed a 'Sopwith Dolphin' near Maserada – this was probably Camel C194, flown by Lt E L Roberts of No 28 Sqn, which was badly shot up on this date. On the 15th, during an escort mission for *Flik* 69/S, Mörath, Grabenhofer and Fw Otto Schrimpl fought with Italian flying boats. A Macchi M.5 of *260ᵗ Squadriglia* was hit and set ablaze, but Sottocapo Emilio Dri was able to alight in Italian waters and escape unhurt, although his fighter was destroyed.

The next day the parachute again showed its utility in a fight between Albatros fighters of *Flik* 61/J and Camels of No 66 Sqn near San Stino di Livenza. Albatros D III 253.65, piloted by Mörath, and 253.59, flown by Zgf Karl Pochobradsky, were shot down by Lt C L Cox in Camel C3288, but the pilots successfully 'hit the silk', although Pochobradsky was wounded.

On 17 September Peter achieved ace status by shooting down Savoia-Pomilio SP.2 PE6886 of *134ª Squadriglia*, whose crew, Sergente Annibale Tonta and Tenente Adriano Barona, perished.

The next success for the Albatros came on 5 October when Bönsch emerged from the fog near Ponte di Piave and, in spite of heavy defensive machine gun fire, attacked a *4ª Sezione* kite balloon, which burst into flames. Two days later, in the Adige Valley, Camel E1498 of No 66 Sqn was shot down by Peter and Zgf Franz Steidl, resulting in the death of 26-year-old Lt George Roy Leighton. On the Piave Front the same fate befell his Canadian squadronmate 2Lt William J Courtenay, who died near San Donà under the fire of Rudorfer of *Flik* 51/J. Another casualty was suffered by No 66 Sqn on the 22nd, although 2Lt James M Kelly, also a Canadian, had more luck and was captured after his Camel, E7167, crashed near San Fior. His demise gave Ujvari his fourth confirmed victory.

On 24 October Italian troops began their last offensive. Kite balloons were again playing a key role in the battle, but in spite of the brave efforts of the *LFT* only one Italian balloon was lost – that of *36ª Sezione*, attacked by a patrol from *Flik* 51/J at 1115 hrs. Rudorfer was able to return, but one of his wingmen, Zgf Josef Pfisterer, was forced to take to his parachute after being hit by ground fire and becoming entangled in the balloon wire.

27 October was a day of hard fighting, which ended with Ujvary becoming an ace after he shared in a victory with Zgf Anton Aussitz near Isola di Papadopoli. Their victim was Lt N H Hamley of No 28 Sqn, who was forced to land Camel E7216. Schrimpl also gained ace status that day when he claimed Caproni Ca.4180 of *2ª Squadriglia*

No wooden structures could resist the wind's fury on 23 September 1918. With its tail broken and nose smashed, D III 253.31 of *Flik* 51/J would never fly again. Zgf Eugen Bönsch had used this aeroplane in the summer, following its delivery in July. To the left is 253.24, flown by Fiala. The Albatros reproduction recently built by Koloman Mayrhofer's Craftlab is in the colours of the latter machine *(Greg VanWyngarden)*

A Caproni gunner with his Fiat 6.5 *mitragliatrice* on the mounting installed over the central pusher engine. From this position he had a very good field-of-fire, but was also completely exposed to the bullets of attacking enemy aircraft. The round grid to the right of the gunner's knees prevented his toes from being hit by the revolving pusher propeller *(Roberto Sardo)*

The war is over. Albatros D III 253.138 and its kin were probably damaged by Austro-Hungarian airmen before their the retreat and then pilfered by souvenir hunters. They will probably soon end up in a bonfire *(Aeronautica Militare Italiana)*

Without weapons, cowlings and tyres, Albatros D III 253.09 was found by Italian troops in a hangar, despite the horseshoe painted on its fuselage. The aeroplane had served with *Flik* 3/J, being flown in July and August by Navratil and in September by Zgf Josef Kopetzky *(Aeronautica Militare Italiana)*

destroyed. The bomber was attacked from above by fighters that came out of the clouds, and although it was hit several times, the aeroplane was able to limp across the lines and land on a British airfield in the middle of Treviso racetrack, with its observer and gunner wounded. The crew in turn asserted that they had shot down one of their adversaries near Sacile, but this claim was not accredited by the Italian command. The Italian airmen were right on this occasion, however, because Albatros D III 153.162 of *Flik* 101/G had indeed crash-landed due to damage from defensive fire.

Schrimpl had joined the *LFT* in February 1916 after serving in one of the *Landesschützenregimentes*. He suffered a serious wound as an observer on 25 November 1916 when his right knee was shattered by a bullet fired from the Nieuport of future ace Tenente Ferruccio Ranza.

In a dogfight near Isola di Papadopoli on 28 October 1918 Bönsch wounded HD 1 pilot Tenente Carlo Pasquinelli of *78ª Squadriglia*. The latter managed to return to his airfield, only to die of his wounds a few days after the war had ended. The next day Bönsch gained his 15th, and last, success, when he claimed a second Hanriot fighter in the same area – a victory that has no corresponding entry in known Allied losses. This proved to be the last claim made by an *LFT* Albatros ace.

Austro-Hungarian air activity was described as 'intense' in the Daily Reports of Italian aviation up until 29 October, after which it was said to be suddenly 'scarce'. Thus was marked the end of a young and brave air force, a gallant 100-year-old army and an ancient and glorious empire.

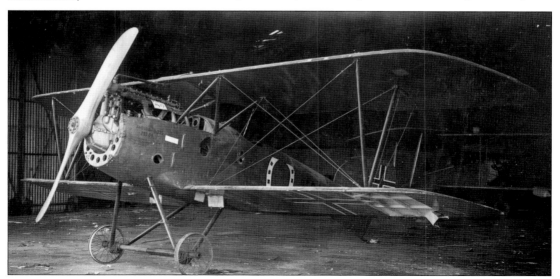

# AFTERMATH

ow citizens of new nations, the soldiers of the dead empire were forced to begin new lives in a wasted world very different from that they had known, having lost almost everything from social status to means of subsistence. The story of the three Perini brothers, gallant pilots during the war, might be considered typical of the fate of the soldiers of this lost war.

Richard, the eldest, became a citizen of the new Austrian Republic, married a Hungarian countess and disappeared during the Hungarian Soviet Republic of Bela Kun in 1919. Kamillo entered the Polish Air Force and joined the famous Kosciuszko Squadron. He left it in 1919 owing to disputes with Marshal Jozef Pilsudski, but in 1940 he played an important role in helping Polish soldiers join General Sikorski in Great Britain by way of neutral Italy. Closely watched by the Italian police, Kamillo did not survive a surgical procedure and died in 1942. Max, the youngest, became an Italian citizen but worked for Daimler in Austria and died testing a car in 1927.

Some airmen were able to continue their careers in the small *Deutschösterreischische Fliegertruppe*, or in the air services of the newly born countries in this region. They often found themselves fighting in new wars, sometimes against old enemies and sometimes against old comrades in new uniforms.

Zgf Adolf Blaha escaped to Switzerland on 21 November 1918, flying from Innsbruck to Schlieren in D III 253.116, which had belonged to Navratil, his commanding officer. The latter pilot had painted the same pierced heart insignia on 253.06 *(Jiri Rajlich)*

Hungarian leanings led Josef von Maier to become a citizen of that country. He changed his name to Joszef Modory and in 1919 fought in the Red Air Corps against Czech, Rumanian and Serbian invaders. In subsequent years he worked for the airline MALERT, donned his uniform again just prior to World War 2 and was finally discharged in 1944 with the rank of colonel.

In 1919 Fejes fought in the 8th Squadron of the Hungarian Red Air Corps, together with Kasza, Udvardy and Riszticz. During a strafing attack near Losoncz (now in Slovakia) in May of that year his Fokker D VII suffered a damaged propeller, which forced him to crash-land and spend six months in captivity. Again with Riszticz, he flew in the first Budapest Airshow in 1920, staging a mock dogfight with his old companion in arms. In 1928 Fejes worked as an instructor in the secret air force that Hungary was setting up in violation of the Trianon Treaty. Among his pupils was future World War 2 ace Aladar de Happes, who described his old teacher to O'Connor thus;

'Fejes gave me my first demonstration flight in 1928. He was a truly superb flier. He spoke in the manner of an educated man. He was a true gentleman and possessed great warmth. He was generally much loved, particularly by the younger students, who called him *Fejes Bacsi* (Uncle Fejes).'

Franz Peter chose to become a Polish citizen and fought against the Ukraine and Soviet Russia prior to being severely wounded on 14 May 1919 during a strafing attack near Kulikovo. He then completed a technical degree, and from 1929 led the engine department of the Institute for Aeronautical Technical Research, becoming technical director of the Avia engine factory in 1932.

Edgar Mörath returned to his chemistry studies and became an engineer.

After a period with Ungarische Luftverkehrs AG, Riszticz joined Junkers as a pilot. In the summer of 1927 he set two world records in a Junkers W 33 – a 65 hrs 25 min endurance flight in July with Wilhelm Zimmermann, followed in August by a distance record with Cornelius Edzard, covering 4660 km (2890 miles) in 52 hrs 22 min. On 14 August 1927 he attempted the first east-west non-stop Atlantic crossing, but the W 33 *Europa* in which he took off with Edzard and the American

**About a year later Blaha set off in 253.116 to join the Republic of Czechoslovakia air force. After some stops en route he reached Prague-Kbely airport, and tried to land in poor weather but crashed. The fighter still bears Navratil's personal insignia, but has had the crosses obliterated and the cockade of the new air service added beneath its wings** *(Jiri Rajlich)*

journalist Knickerbocker was dogged by bad weather and engine problems. Riszticz then took part in two International Touring Aircraft Contests, flying in both the 1929 and 1930 Challenges.

Although Hungarian-born, Riszticz had acquired fluent Serbian from his father, a Serbian orthodox priest. His linguistic ability surprised everyone when, in 1932, he flew to Belgrade in a Junkers G 24 for the Royal Yugoslavian Air Force.

Pilots like Kaszala, Hautzmayer and Hefty found work as flying instructors or with the early airlines. Magerl had left the front in March 1918, and spent the rest of the war instructing at the Campoformido flying school. After the conflict had ended he worked in the *Flughafenpolizei* at Aspern, then for the Austrian airline ÖLAG and, eventually, Lufthansa after the 1938 Anschluss.

Some of the aces who had flown Albatros fighters eventually met their deaths in the cockpit . Karl Nikitsch ended the war as commanding officer of the *Flieger-Lehr-Batallions* (Aviation Training Battalions) in Wiener Neustadt. He died in a flying accident on 7 September 1927, and two days later the Austrian newspaper *Tage-Post* published the following obituary;

'Director of Airport Police Hptm(ret.) and *Polizeirat* Dr Karl Nikitsch crashed yesterday afternoon at 1750 hrs on Aspern airfield and was killed immediately. They had taken off in a French biplane when, suddenly, the engine seized, causing the aircraft to turn quickly, fall away on its left wing and crash to the ground. Dr Nikitsch was crushed to death in the wreck of the aeroplane. He was 42 years old, and as an airman during the war had been shot down several times and suffered several fractures of his arms and legs. Previously a simple policeman, he completed law studies and graduated from the University of Graz.'

In November 1918 Raoul Stojsavljevic, who first had to recover from the wounds he had suffered in the January crash of Brandenburg C I 68.07, commanded the Officer Flying School in Wiener Neustadt. He chose Austrian nationality, resisting General Uzelac's direct invitation to join the new Yugoslavian air force, and like Nikitsch he served in the new air forces of the Republic. In 1925, still suffering from the thighbone injury caused by an enemy bullet seven years before, 'Iron Stoj' retired from the military, but not from aviation, working to establish Innsbruck Airport. A crash in 1927 did not stop him flying, and a year later he joined the Austrian airline ÖLAG as a commercial pilot. On 2 September 1930 Stojsavljevic was flying alone from Innsbruck to Zürich, in Switzerland, in Junkers F 13 A-3 *Taube* when, over Bavaria, the aeroplane entered a thick fog bank and crashed into the Krottenkopf massif, north of Garmisch-Partenkirchen.

Karl Kaszala was given a Brandenburg B I as a gesture of appreciation when he left the Aero Club of the Hungarian Technical University of Budapest, of which he had been a founding member. With this aircraft, registered H-MAFG, he earned his living flying in airshows with his wife, who was also a pilot. During an exhibition on 4 September 1932 the Brandenburg spun in from low altitude and crashed to the ground, killing Kaszala and his passenger, Janos Urbaschek.

Ludwig Hautzmayer, who had married a Hungarian woman and changed his German name to Lajos Tataj, met his death on 9 December

1936 while taking off from Croydon Airport, near London, in KLM Douglas DC-2 PH-AKL. Among the passengers who also died was Juan de la Cierva, the pioneer of the autogyro.

The Austro-Hungarian 'ace of aces' died that same year. Godwin Brumowski had decided to retire immediately after the war, and was discharged on 13 February 1919 with an annual pension of 1360 *Kronen*. The ace, who in 1918 had married Marianne Kaiser, lived initially in Kaiserstrasse 59 in Vienna, but later moved to Transylvania to live on his mother-in-law's estate. The life of the country gentleman was not for Brumowski, however, and he tried to escape boredom and overcome his sadness by riding horses, driving fast cars, hunting in the mountains and skiing. In the 1930s he finally returned to Vienna and remarried, going back to the only world to which he felt he belonged. In 1931 he was among the financial backers and pilots of Österreichische Phoenix-Flugzeugwerft Ges.m.b.H., a company that built light aeroplanes. A year later he made a noteworthy flight over the Alps, making takeoffs and landings on the snow.

The political and social climate of Austria in those years was very volatile owing to contrasts between socialists and conservatives, which often turned into bloody street fights. The political opinions of Brumowski, like those of many former soldiers not only in Austria, tended to be right-wing, and the ace duly joined the *Heimwehr* – a paramilitary association like the German *Freikorps*. On 12-16 February 1934 the politically inspired fighting in Austria reached new heights, with violent clashes taking place in several cities. On 14 February Brumowski made the only air attack of the so-called *Februarkämpfe* (Battle of February), strafing the Goethe-Hof in Vienna in which the socialists were barricaded. It is a sad truth that the last bullets fired by the great ace were aimed at his fellow countrymen.

**The wreck of Miles M 3B Falcon Six OE-DVH, in which Godwin Brumowski and Dutch banker Adrianus Van Hengel perished following their failed landing attempt at Schiphol airport, Amsterdam, during the afternoon of 3 June 1936 (Herman Dekker)**

In 1935 Brumowski helped found the *Österreichischen Fliegerschule* in Vienna with fellow veteran Hans Löw, who would become a senior Luftwaffe officer during World War 2.

That same year Adrianus Van Hengel, the Dutch banker chosen by the Austrian government to lead the Credit-Anstalt bank after the world economic crisis, joined the school. Van Hengel took flying lessons with his wife and bought a Miles M 3B Falcon Six in the UK, Brumowski flying it from the manufacturer's Berkshire factory to Austria in November 1935. In May 1936 the Österreichischen Aero Club organised a race in several stages from Graz to Basel, Switzerland. Van Hengel entered the competition in the Miles, now registered OE-DVH, while Brumowski flew with the businessman's wife, Helena, in British Aircraft Manufacturing Co Swallow OE-SSD (a Klemm L 25 licence-built in Britain).

On 3 June 1936, immediately after arriving in Basel, Van Hengel took off in the Falcon Six with Brumowski in the passenger seat. About three hours later the monoplane was approaching Schiphol Airport near Amsterdam. After a wide left turn the Miles stalled at a height of about 200 m (650 ft), spun and crashed. The rescuers could only extricate the bodies of the occupants, who had not fastened their seat belts and had died from fractures and internal wounds. The enquiry revealed that the aeroplane, which had had its baggage compartment enlarged, was overloaded, and that its centre of gravity was outside safe limits. Brumowski was still very famous, and several hundred people crowded Vienna railway station to pay a last tribute to his body, which was then buried in the *Zentralfriedhof*.

Austria was annexed to Germany in 1938, by which time war clouds were again gathering over Europe. When World War 2 broke out in September 1939, several former aces had been called up to serve in Germany's Luftwaffe. *Diplomingenieur* Mörath served in air transport units and became a *Gruppenkommandeur*. Arigi became commanding officer of the Schwechat fighter pilot school, near Vienna, and had among his pupils future aces Joachim Marseille and Walter Nowotny. Lahner and Bönsch also donned uniforms again, the former leaving his lumber business and the latter his inn in Bohemia to become director of Oschatz airfield in Saxony. Riszticz test-flew aeroplanes for a maintenance plant in Breslau, while Benno Fiala von Fernbrugg commanded Linz Hörsching airfield.

After World War 1 Fiala had taken advantage of his technical background, and in 1921 he worked for the Moewe Werft at Aspen. He continued his studies at Vienna Technical University, where in 1923 he graduated as *Diplomingenieur*. In August 1925 he started working with Professor Hugo Junkers as manager of his maintenance plant in Fürth. Fiala then moved to Warsaw to direct maintenance with *Polska Linja Lotnicza Aerolot*, an appointment he held until 1927. In the following years Fiala travelled to the United States and Japan, before eventually becoming chief engineer for Junkers.

In 1933 the new Nazi government started manoeuvring to gain control of the company. The first step was to place Hugo Junkers, who was beset by financial problems, under partial arrest, and force him to transfer his private patent rights. Fiala was also arrested and held for three days. For Hugo Junkers the ordeal had only just begun. He was forced to relinquish the control of his company completely, and died at home on 3 February 1935 – the date of his 76th birthday – whilst still under arrest. Fiala, who had retained his Austrian citizenship, returned to Vienna. Still working as an engineer, he also founded the Wiener Neustadt Airport Management Association with Julius Arigi.

As a Polish citizen, Franz Peter again found himself on the losing side in 1939. Evacuated to France, he worked for Hispano-Suiza, but in 1941 he was forced to return to Poland and work for the German war effort. He also taught at Warsaw Technical University.

Friedrich Hefty spent the war as a lieutenant in the Correspondence Unit of the Royal Hungarian Air Force. Immediately after the end of World War 1 he had fought in the new Hungarian air force against Rumanians, Serbs and Czechs. He had then flown for Air France and MALERT, later establishing flying schools in Hungary and Egypt. Fellow ace Fejes also worked for MALERT at this time, and during World War 2 he flew transport and liaison aircraft.

Navratil attained the highest position of all the aces. He served in the Yugoslav Air Force as a colonel, and in 1943 left Budapest, where he was military attaché, to become Minister of the Armed Forces in the Nazi puppet state known as the Independent State of Croatia. The Ustasha leader Ante Pavelic found the old airman too friendly toward the Serbs and removed him in January 1944, but this was not enough to save his life when accounts were settled at the end of World War 2. Navratil was captured in Austria by American troops and sent to Yugoslavia in December 1946. There, he was found guilty of war crimes and executed on 7 June 1947. Meanwhile, Kasza had lost his life along with his whole family in Budapest during a Russian air raid in February 1945.

When peace returned, the surviving airmen went home to rebuild their lives once again in yet another world. Bönsch found employment in the inn managed by his brother in Ehrwald, in the Tyrol, spoke no more of the wars he had seen and died on 24 July 1951. Magerl passed away on 25 July 1954 in Vienna, and Maier (or Modory) died that same year. Fiala returned to Vienna to work as chief designer for a manufacturing company, and he passed away in the Austrian capital on 29 October 1964. Three years later the *Österreichische Luftstreitkräfte* air base of Aigen, in Ennstal, was named Fliegerhorst Fiala-Fernbrugg in his honour. In 1968 the airport was used for some scenes in the film *Where Eagles Dare*, having been given the phoney name of 'Oberhausen'.

After his release from prison, Hefty found it hard to live with the new political climate in Hungary and emigrated to the USA, where he settled in Detroit and died on 20 January 1965. Mörath returned to engineering until his death in February 1969, aged 71, and Lahner sold lumber in Linz, where, after a severe cerebral stroke, he passed away on 19 July 1966 aged 73. Peter died in Warsaw two years later and Johann Ristics passed away in the city of Duisburg, in Germany, on 7 January 1973. Arigi returned to civilian life and remained active until old age. At 77 he took advantage of his previous work experience to rewire his house. Arigi was the last to join his old comrades, dying peacefully in his sleep on 1 August 1981 in his house in Attersee. His personal letterhead bore two winged hands clasped together under the Latin word for peace – PAX.

# APPENDICES

## Victory claims

Each air service involved in World War 1 had its own rules to define an 'aerial victory', and even internal valuation methods sometimes differed slightly over time. If a smouldering wreck burnt on one's own side of the lines left little room for doubt, in the majority of cases the term 'victory' had a very broad meaning. This could range from the actual destruction of an enemy aircraft to it being generically 'driven off', perhaps in unusual attitudes that could be interpreted as 'out of control', but which more often than not were extreme evasive manoeuvres. In this war, as in all others, so-called 'overclaiming' was common to every air force.

Generally speaking, the victory confirmation system within a given air service was the same, even allowing for little differences in relation to the period or front. This means that the relative effectiveness between airmen of the same air force can be compared throughout the war with a certain degree of accuracy. An easy comparison might be the distance between Paris and Rome, which remains the same regardless of whether it is expressed in kilometres, miles or Persian parasangs. The only difference is its numerical expression. Conversely, any comparison between numbers produced by completely different confirmation systems borders on the meaningless, to say nothing of other significant variables such as the number of flights, aeroplanes available, encounters with the enemy and so on.

What appears to be very useful to know is what actually happened in those distant skies, and to cross-check the claims with the actual recorded losses. This task has now been made possible through the study of primary sources kept in the archives of the countries involved in World War 1, which in most cases allow individual events to be reconstructed.

A detailed explanation of the rules by which the Austro-Hungarian air service (Army and Navy) confirmed or denied a claim is well beyond the limits of this work. In general it can be said that the system was based on very loose criteria, which, supported by the optimistic reports of the ground observers, confirmed as 'victories' aircraft that had actually escaped with minor or no damage. This conclusion is not based on unreasonable and superficial chauvinism, but rather on an objective and extensive examination of what actually happened, with the aim of gaining a better understanding of the true balance of power, and of the true results achieved by both sides.

In this respect the author wishes to emphasise that he shares in the judgment of the Austro-Hungarian airmen by leading Italian ace Francesco Baracca, who described them as being 'very gallant' in a letter he wrote during the height of the conflict.

In 1927 Ltn Ladislaus Hauser wrote an article that was quoted by Richard Cavigioli in his pioneering work about the *LFT's* wartime experiences on the Italian front. Hauser noted;

'The mistakes, missed opportunities and the insurmountable difficulties that often hindered the work of the Austro-Hungarian pilots are now becoming visible, but this underscores even more the merits of the small number of aviators who fulfilled their duty, fighting against much larger forces, despite all the difficulties, faithfully, until the last moment. If Austro-Hungarian pilots did not always achieve the desired success, the fault is not theirs.'

## Aces and Victories

The *K u K Luftfahrtruppen* did not issue an official list of its aces, although victories and numbers were often given in official documents. Historians who have researched the subject since World War 1 reached conclusions that agreed in general terms, but there are still some discrepancies in several cases about the correct number of victories officially homologated at that time and the aeroplanes in which they were obtained. The author believes it could be useful to list the total numbers given by the most reliable, recent and known historians. Obviously, the pilots who did not gain at least one victory flying the Albatros D II or D III are excluded from the list.

| Name | Total number of victories | | | Victories on Albatros fighters | | |
|---|---|---|---|---|---|---|
| | Meindl | O'Connor | Tesar | Meindl | O'Connor | Tesar |
| Godwin Brumowski | 39 | 35 | 35 | 16 | 16 | 16 |
| Julius Arigi | * | 32 | 32 | * | 13 | 13 |
| Benno Fiala von Fernbrugg | 28 | 28 | 28 | 20 | 20 | 20 |
| Frank Linke-Crawford | 30 | 27 | 27 | 10 | 9 | 9 |
| Josef Kiss | 19 | 19 | 19 | 12 | 12 | 12 |
| Franz Gräser | 20 | 18 | 18 | 16 | 16 | 17 |
| Eugen Bönsch | 16 | 16 | 16 | 16 | 16 | 16 |
| Stefan Fejes | 16 | 16 | 16 | 10 | 11 | 11 |
| Ernst Strohschneider | 15 | 15 | 15 | 13 | About 10 | About 10 |
| Kurt Gruber | 11 | 11 | 11 | 2 | Unknown | Probably 2 |
| Franz Rudorfer | 12 | Not listed | 11 | 11 | Not listed | 10 |
| Friedrich Navratil | 10 | 10 | 10 | 10 | 10 | 10 |
| Raoul Stoisavljevic | 13 | 10 | 10 | At least 1 | Probably 1 | Probably 1 |
| Georg von Kenzian | 9 | 9 | 9 | 7 | 7 | 7 |
| Karl Kaszala | 8 | 8 | 8 | 3 | 3 | 3 |
| Alexander Tahy | 8 | 8 | 8 | 3 | 3 | 3 |
| Ferdinand Udvardy | 8 | 8 | 8 | At least 5 | At least 2 | At least 2 |
| Josef Friedrich | 9 | 7 | 7 | 2 | 2 | 2 |
| Ludwig Hautzmayer | 7 | 7 | 7 | 4 | 4 | 4 |
| Otto Jäger | 7 | 7 | 7 | 2 | 2 | 2 |
| Josef von Maier | 7 | 7 | 7 | 7 | 7 | 7 |
| Johann Riszticz | 7 | 7 | 7 | 2 | At least 2 | At least 2 |
| Andreas Dombrowski | 6 | 6 | 6 | 1 | 1 | 1 |
| Alexander Kasza | 6 | 6 | 6 | 4 | At least 4 | At least 4 |
| Karl Nikitsch | 6 | 6 | 6 | 3 | At least 3 | At least 3 |
| Franz Peter | 6 | 6 | 6 | 6 | 6 | 6 |
| Wedige von Froreich | 5 | Not listed | 5 | 3 | Not listed | 3 |
| Friedrich Hefty | 5 | 5 | 5 | 3 | 3 | 3 |
| Julius Kowalczik | 5 | 5 | 5 | 2 | 1 | 1 |
| Franz Lahner | 5 | 5 | 5 | 5 | 5 | 5 |
| Vinzenz Magerl | 5 | Not listed | 5 | ? | Not listed | At least 1 |
| Franz Oberst | 4 | Not listed | 5 | 4 | Not listed | 5 |
| Karl Patzelt | 5 | 5 | 5 | 3 | ? | ? |
| Rudolf Szepessy-Sokoll | 5 | 5 | 5 | 4 | 4 | 4 |
| Karl Teichmann | 5 | 5 | 5 | Probably 2 | ? | ? |
| Edgar Morath | 6 | Not listed | 4 | 6 | Not listed | 4 |
| Otto Schrimpl | 5 | Not listed | 4 | 5 | Not listed | 4 |
| Lajos Telessy | 5 | Not listed | 4 | 3 | Not listed | 3 |
| Ladislaus Ujvari | 5 | Not listed | Not listed | 5 | Not listed | Not listed |

* The Austrian historian's volume covering the Albanian Front is not yet published.

The sources used for this table are as follows:

Meindl, Karl, *Die Luftsiege der K u K Luftfahrtruppen*, 2005

O'Connor, Martin, *Air Aces of the Austro-Hungarian Empire,* Champlin Fighter Museum Press, Falcon Field, 1986

Tesar, Peter Aharon, *Albatros D II & D III*, JaPo, Hradec Kralove, 1998

## 1

### Albatros D III 53.24 of *Flik* 31 and *Kampfstaffel Harja*, Harja, autumn 1917

This early D III arrived on the Eastern Front in the summer of 1917 and flew in plain finish until late August of the same year, when all the aircraft of the 1st Army Sector in Transylvania had their wingtips painted black. Originally, the Eiserne Kreuz (Iron Cross) on the fuselage sides had the standard white outline, but some photographs show that this was blackened in operational use and then the whole cross was erased, as seen here, leaving only a light 'shadow' on the darker plywood background. Four different pilots claimed single victories with 53.24, making it the most successful fighter in Rumania. The D III was then moved to Italy, where it served with the Campoformido Feldfliegerschule in 1918.

## 2

### Albatros D III 53.27 of Hptm Godwin Brumowski, *Flik* 41/J, Sesana, June 1917

The spinners of this production series were often removed to prevent in-flight structural failure. The aeroplane shows a camouflage scheme typical of the unit, devised by Brumowski according to some sources, and applied in the field. Over the plain finish the fighter received a coat of dark green on the uppersurfaces of the wings, the upper part of the fuselage, the tailplane, fin, rudder, engine cowling, spinner and wheel discs. Except for the metal parts of the nose cowling, on this green background were applied yellowish 'tresses'. The struts were painted black. As usual for LFT Albatros scouts, the aircraft's serial number was painted in black onto its fuselage using a template, the digits being 250 mm high and 95 mm wide. Flik 41 marked its aircraft with black-and-white symbols – Albatros scouts sometimes inherited insignias previously used on KD fighters. The three-pointed black-and-white star on 53.27 had been seen before on the fuselage of Brandenburg D I 28.10. This D III was later used by Flik 42/J prior to ending its days with the Wiener Neustadt Fliegeroffiziersschule.

## 3

### Albatros D III 53.30 of *Flik* 6/F, Tirana, June 1917

The 'Jolly Roger' applied to 53.30 stands out against the fighter's otherwise plain finish. The insignia was possibly created by Oblt Karl Benedek. As usual for the Albatros, on the wooden nose panel there is the factory logo – a black-and-white triangle with a stylised bird (or aeroplane) and the word Öffag. The insignia was applied on either side of the forward fuselage. Due to the shortage of synchronisation systems, D III 53.30 was initially fitted with an upper-wing Schwarzlose machine gun. Following a crash on 26 August 1917 the aircraft was repaired and fitted with a synchronised gun. In the spring of 1918 it was flown by ace Off Stv Julius Arigi.

## 4

### Albatros D III 53.60 of Fw Kurt Gruber, *Flik* 41/J, Sesana, summer 1917

Like 53.27, this aeroplane had the typical camouflage finish applied to Flik 41/J machines for much of 1917. It bears a black-and-white crescent with a six-pointed star on the fuselage sides, and on top of the fuselage, just aft of the cockpit, it appears that only the star is repeated in black. The crescent and star had already been seen on KD 28.13. Aside from Gruber, Fw Hermann Richter and Kpl Ignaz Pillwein also saw combat in this machine. Indeed, 53.60 had a long life, and following service with Flik 2 in October 1918 it was sent to the Wiener-Neustadt Luftfahrzeugabwehrstation. The fighter survived the war and was offered for sale in 1920.

## 5

### Albatros D III series 153 (serial unknown) of StFw Johann Riszticz, *Flik* 42/J, Pianzano, spring/summer 1918

*Flik* 42/J often removed the serial numbers of its Albatros fighters during the last summer of the war, and with some exceptions only a black-bordered red (or white) digit identified most of the unit's aircraft. All aeroplanes assigned to *Flik* 42/J featured red-and-white wheel discs.

## 6

### Albatros D III 153.06 of Hptm Godwin Brumowski, *Flik* 41/J, Sesana, summer 1917

Brumowski obtained his first two confirmed D III victories with this aeroplane on 19 and 20 August 1917 when he downed two Italian reconnaissance aircraft during the first days of the 11th Isonzo Battle. 153.06, finished in the individual camouflage of *Flik* 41/J, sports another example of the elegant black-and-white insignia that adorned fighters of this unit, completely obliterating the serial. By 26 September 1917 this fighter had been sent in an engineless state to Flep 6, and it was written off a month later.

## 7

### Albatros D III 153.10 of Hptm Godwin Brumowski, *Flik* 41/J, Torresella, winter 1917

In the case of 153.10, the insignia obscures only part of the serial number. This Albatros was used by Brumowski for a patrol that lasted 1 hr 20 min on 16 December 1917 – his last operational flight of the year. D III 153.10 was subsequently flown by Oblt Gustav von Salmon in March 1918.

## 8

### Albatros D III 153.11 of Oblt Frank Linke-Crawford, *Flik* 41/J, Torresella, winter 1917

A majestic bird of prey spreads its wings on the fuselage of the fighter flown by Linke-Crawford, who also had his insignia painted on D III 153.16. It is possible that some details of the insignia were coloured, as shown in this profile. The ace claimed victories with this aeroplane on 23 October, 5 November (a double) and 23 November 1917. Zgf Alfred Brandt escaped unhurt from the wreck of 153.11 on 26 December 1917 after a dogfight with Sergente Ennio Sorrentino of 81a Squadriglia.

## 9

### Albatros D III series 153 (serial unknown) of StFw Karl Kaszala, *Flik* 41/J, Sesana, summer 1917

This fighter, perhaps 153.12, was adorned with a black-and-white comet on its fuselage sides. Owing to the aircraft's lack of synchronisation gear, a Schwarzlose machine gun was fixed to a mounting and angled to fire outside the propeller arc. If the identification of the serial number is correct, this Albatros was also flown by Brumowski on at least one mission in October 1917. It was written off in November of the same year.

## 10

**Albatros D III 153.24 of Oblt Hans Fischer, *Kampfstaffel Galanesti*, Galanesti, October 1917**

This plain-finish Albatros served with *Kampfstaffel Galanesti* and *Kampfstaffel Harja*. It was one of only a handful of D IIIs, if not the only one, committed to combat on the Eastern Front to carry a personal insignia. The six-pointed black-and-white star was repeated on the top and bottom of the fuselage.

## 11

**Albatros D III 153.27 of Oblt Georg von Kenzian, *Flik* 55/J, Pergine, November 1917**

An official document signed by Hptm von Maier in November 1917 attests that all *Flik* 55/J aircraft had blue-green uppersurfaces and light blue undersurfaces. On this particular machine the wing struts and undercarriage were also painted in these colours. The pennant chosen as a personal insignia had a blue section outlined in white and a white section outlined in blue. Kenzian claimed two of his nine victories with this aircraft, on 18 and 27 November 1917. After being damaged in a crash-landing at Pergine airfield in December of the same year due to a mechanical failure, D.III 153.27 was written off the following January.

## 12

**Albatros D III 153.29 of Fw Stefan Fejes, *Flik* 51/J, Ajdussina, autumn 1917**

This machine, which had its spinner removed, bore Fejes' six-pointed star marking that duly became the insignia of the whole unit. In 1918 the Albatros was handed over to the Campoformido *Feldfliegerschule*, and some photographs show that the insignia was complemented by a wolf's head painted on the fuselage beside the cockpit.

## 13

**Albatros D III 153.33 of *Rittmeister* Wedige von Froreich, *Flik* 51/J, Ajdussina, autumn 1917**

This fighter arrived in plain finish at the front, where a dark green camouflage with yellowish dots was added to the rudder only. The red-and-white pennant was Froreich's personal insignia, the five-victory ace leading the unit during the autumn of 1917. He flew this aircraft in September and October of that year, and the following December it suffered an in-flight engine failure and was written off.

## 14

**Albatros D III 153.42 of StFw Ferdinand Udvardy, *Flik* 42/J, Prosecco, October 1917**

The blinding white plain-fabric finish of new D IIIs arriving from the factory was criticised by *Flik* 42/J's commanding officer, Hptm Ladislaus Hary, in his monthly report. Nonetheless, it seems that this aircraft was left unpainted, the pilot adding only his personal insignia to either side of the fuselage in the

form a black-edged red heart. Albatros D III 153.42 had been transferred to the *Materialdepot* (Material Store) at Aspern by March 1918, and it survived the war and was offered for sale to the Czechoslovak Republic in 1920.

## 15

**Albatros D III 153.44 of Ltn Franz Gräser, *Flik* 42/J, Motta di Livenza, late autumn 1917**

StFw Hefty saw combat in this aeroplane in October 1917, but it was Gräser who gained four confirmed victories with the fighter on 23, 27 and 28 November and 5 December. Boldly painted onto the aircraft's overall plain finish is an eagle owl, which was chosen by Gräser as his personal insignia. The D III also has the distinctive red-and-white wheel discs of *Flik* 42/J. 153.44 was repaired in the Aspern workshop in early 1918, after which it was returned to the Italian Front for a second tour of duty, assigned to the 6th Army.

## 16

**Albatros D III 153.45 of Hptm Godwin Brumowski, *Flik* 41/J, Torresella, November 1917**

Inspired by Manfred von Richthofen, Brumowski chose a red overall finish for his personal mount, adding a white skull shrouded in black on the sides and top of the fuselage. He claimed eight victories in this aircraft from October 1917 to April 1918. According to an interview given by the ace's daughter, Brumowski's gruesome insignia could have been emblematic of his attitude toward life, which he saw as a continuous challenge against danger and death.

## 17

**Albatros D III 153.47 of StFw Josef Kiss, *Flik* 55/J, Pergine, January 1918**

This aeroplane had blue-green uppersurfaces, light blue undersurfaces and black struts. Black-and-white numbers or letters were typical of *Flik* 55/J from November 1917, often in conjunction with other markings. For example, Kiss adopted the number '7' with a white band, Arigi a '5' with a white capital 'X' and von Maier, as commanding officer, had a '1'. Kiss claimed four victories with D III 153.47, which was then transferred to *Flik* 9/J. It was the mount of Fw Michael Meissner when he was shot down and killed on 19 June 1918.

## 18

**Albatros D III 153.52 of Hptm Godwin Brumowski, *Flik* 41/J, Torresella, winter 1917**

With this fighter the ace introduced a variation to his favourite plumage, adding dense tresses of a lighter colour to the overall red finish. The struts were black, while the yellow wheel discs with black centres were a unit-wide marking introduced in October 1917 and briefly used by *Flik* 41/J. 153.52 was badly damaged on 4 February 1918 during combat with British fighters, but Brumowski was able to crash-land near Passerella and extricate himself from the overturned Albatros without injury. He had previously claimed two victories in D III 153.52, on 28 November and 13 December 1917.

## 19

**Albatros D III 153.106 of Ltn Franz Gräser, *Flik* 61/J, Motta di Livenza, March 1918**

Gräser also had his personal insignia applied to this aircraft, which was camouflaged in dark brown overall bar the metal parts of the forward fuselage. These were left in natural metal. The fighter also sported the red wheel discs of *Flik* 61/J. According to some sources the dark finish on some *Flik* 61/J aeroplanes was applied for experimental night flights by the unit's commanding officer, Oblt Strohschneider. Five victories were claimed by Gräser with this machine from January to March 1918, and 153.106 was also flown in May 1918 by fellow ace Oblt Ludwig Hautzmayer.

## 20
### Albatros D III 153.119 of Oblt Ernst Strohschneider, *Flik* 61/J, Motta di Livenza, March 1918

Strohschneider's personal insignia was a red heart outlined in white. Like 153.106, this aircraft was painted dark brown except for the metal parts of the nose, and it too had red wheel discs. The ace claimed three victories flying this Albatros, on 24 February and 16 and 27 March 1918. Oblt Ludwig Hautzmayer also used this machine in May of the same year. 153.119 was written off the following September.

## 21
### Albatros D III 153.140 of Zgf Eugen Bönsch, *Flik* 51/J, Ghirano, spring 1918

The plain finish of 153.140 was enhanced by a black-outlined red twin-tailed arrow on each side of the fuselage. This aeroplane was delivered by Oeffag in January 1918 and sent to *Flik* 51/J, based at Ghirano airfield. Bönsch claimed victories in it on 16 March, 17 April and 20 June 1918. In June and July the aircraft was flown by Kpl Josef Pfisterer, but it was written off after suffering wing failure the following month.

## 22
### Albatros D III 153.141 of Ltn Franz Rudorfer, *Flik* 51/J, Ghirano, summer 1918

Another variant of the six-pointed star used by *Flik* 51/J distinguished this aeroplane. The emblem, outlined in black and white, is halved diagonally in two colours, possibly red and yellow. After surviving the Armistice, D III 153.140 was stored in a depot on Aspern airfield through to March 1919.

## 23
### Albatros D III 153.144 of Ltn Franz Gräser, *Flik* 61/J, Motta di Livenza, February 1918

While the dark brown Albatros of *Flik* 61/J had only red wheel discs as unit markings, the plain-finished aircraft of the same unit also bore stripes in this colour on their wings and tails, as depicted here. This Albatros also served with *Flik* 63/J.

## 24
### Albatros D III 153.169 of StFw Friedrich Hefty, *Flik* 42/J, Pianzano, June 1918

This plain-finish Albatros had the red-and-white wheel discs and large red-and-black digits typical of aircraft assigned to *Flik* 42/J. In this case, however, the colours of the digits were reversed on either side of the fuselage, and the fuselage was also adorned with the pilot's personal insignia. For the latter,

Hefty chose two green shields with a crown, which on one side bore the letter 'G', the significance of which is unknown, and on the other an 'I', standing for Ilonka, the name of his sweetheart.

## 25
### Albatros D III Series 153 (serial unknown) of Oblt Josef von Maier, *Flik* 55/J, Pergine, May 1918

The serial number of this fighter (possibly 153.185) was covered by camouflage, which seems to be a thick overlapping of dark green and grey-green mottles dabbed on a light background. The undersurfaces were light blue. The fuselage number in black and white was chosen as a personal insignia by Maier, who later flew aeroplanes identified by a capital 'M'. On 4 April 1918, D III 153.185 was successfully crash-landed on Ospedaletto airfield following wing failure in flight.

## 26
### Albatros D III Series 153 (serial unknown) of Offz Stv Josef Kiss, *Flik* 55/J, Pergine, March 1918

On this D III too, the serial (probably 153.186) was covered by dark green and grey-green mottle camouflage over a light background. The undersurfaces were light blue, like the struts, which had grey-green mottled finish. The fighter's 'medal' insignia was applied in red and blue, over which was painted a white 'K'. This aircraft was also flown by Kpl Otto Kullas and Oblt Josef Kos. 153.186 was lost when it crashed into Lake Caldonazzo on 5 August 1918, killing its pilot, StFw Karl Greischberger.

## 27
### Albatros D III 153.198 of Oblt Friedrich Navratil, *Flik* 3/J, Romagnano, August 1918

The field camouflage of this Albatros possibly consisted of two shades of dark green dabbed on a lighter background, while the undersurfaces were probably left unpainted. Flying this machine, Navratil claimed the unit's first victory on 28 June 1918. In July the aircraft crashed upon landing at Romagnano airfield.

## 28
### Albatros D III 153.209 of Oblt Godwin Brumowski, *Flik* 41/J, Portobuffolè, June 1918

The last red aeroplane flown by Brumowski in combat during the war was fitted with a captured British Aldis gunsight – these were highly valued by German and Austro-Hungarian airmen, who actively sought to retrieve them from wrecked aircraft. This Albatros was used by the ace to claim his last victory, on 20 June 1918, when he fought over the Montello with an Italian SIA.7b reconnaissance aeroplane. Following Brumowski's departure from the front, D III 153.209 was flown by Kpl Julius Trojan.

## 29
### Albatros D III 253.05 of Oblt Franz Peter, *Flik* 3/J, Romagnano, August 1918

Two shades of dark green over a lighter background camouflage this the aeroplane, flown by Peter. The ace adopted a red-and-white Yin and Yang symbol as his personal insignia. The wings, tailplane and rudder were covered with printed swirled fabric produced by the J Backhausen & Sohne factory in Vienna. Peter shot down the SVA aircraft of Sergente Giovanni Bartolomeo Arrigoni (a four-victory pilot) with this aeroplane on 4 August 1918, the Italian being killed in action near Aldeno during a reconnaissance mission.

## 30
### Albatros D III 253.06 of Oblt Friedrich Navratil, *Flik* 3/J, Romagnano, August 1918

This aircraft was camouflaged by applying dark green and grey-green mottling with a sponge onto a light grey/yellow background. The new straight-armed national insignia (the *Balkenkreuz*), introduced in July, was applied only to the rudder. The red heart pierced by a white arrow was also used on 253.116, which Navratil flew during the last months of the war. It was eventually flown in Switzerland by Zgf Adolf Blaha after the Armistice.

## 31
### Albatros D III 253.12 of Oblt Ludwig Hautzmayer, *Flik* 61/J, Ghirano, summer 1918

This plain-finish aircraft was assigned to Hautzmayer towards the end of the war. It had the red rudder stripes and red wheel discs peculiar to *Flik* 61/J machines. The aircraft's metal panels appear

to be painted in a dark colour, probably the same red. The pennant on the fuselage side, outlined in black, seems to be in white and a darker colour, perhaps blue. This aircraft was severely damaged while landing on Portobuffolè airfield on 4 October 1918, but its pilot, Ltn Henryk Skoczdopole, escaped unscathed.

## 32
### Albatros D III 253.31 of Zgf Eugen Bönsch, *Flik* 51/J, Ghirano, September 1918

Note this aircraft's 'data plate' on its nose beneath the Oeffag logo. According to a rule introduced in 1917, the first two rows of the data block contained the machine's type designation and its serial number in 50 mm letters. The following rows gave the empty weight, the quantity of petrol, oil and water carried and, finally, the payload in 20 mm letters and digits. In July and August 1918 Bönsch fought in this plain-finished Albatros, identified by yet another version of his six-pointed star. On 23 September 1918, 253.11 was destroyed in its hangar on Ghirano airfield, along with other aircraft, when a hurricane of unusual violence wrought havoc on that part of Italy, hitting the opposing sides impartially. Like many other *LFT* aeroplanes, this aircraft still bore the old-style national insignia at the time of its destruction.

# INDEX